"In *Tex-Mex*, Ford takes us to the place he was born and raised to show us a visionary guide to that timeless cooking and disclosing the secrets to what I call 'the other Southern cuisine.' It is a revelatory book that will make you want to heartily wander the border." —HUGH ACHESON

"Ford Fry's food is warm, inviting, and soulful, and his passion for all things Tex-Mex—from queso to combo plates—is contagious. If you love refried beans, salsa, enchiladas, and tacos, you'll want to cook everything in this beautiful and lively new book. I know I'll be referring to it time and time again." —LISA FAIN

"These authors make the perfect team to capture the crave-ability of Tex-Mex. This fantastic book will lead you to discover the soul of Texas's ultimate comfort food." —TYSON COLE

"The photos and recipes make you salivate and the stories remind you of the friends and family who you've shared a basket of warm chips and salsa with countless times before. I for one plan to enjoy this book the way it was meant to be: with a big bowl of queso dip in front of me and an ice-cold margarita in hand!" —KEVIN GILLESPIE

TEX
MEX

TRADITIONS, INNOVATIONS, *and* *Comfort Foods* FROM BOTH SIDES OF THE BORDER

FORD FRY

AND JESSICA DUPUY

PHOTOGRAPHS BY JOHNNY AUTRY

TEX MEX

CLARKSON POTTER/
PUBLISHERS
NEW YORK

Library of Congress Cataloging-in-Publication Data
Names: Fry, Ford, author. | Dupuy, Jessica, author. |
    Autry, Johnny, photographer.
Title: Tex-Mex : traditions, innovations, and comfort
    foods from both sides of the border / Ford Fry with
    Jessica Dupuy ; photographs by Johnny Autry.
Description: First edition. | New York : Clarkson Potter/
    Publishers, 2019. | Includes index.
Identifiers: LCCN 2018032936 | ISBN 9780525573869
    (hardcover)
Subjects: LCSH: Mexican American cooking. | Cooking,
    American—Southwestern style. | LCGFT: Cookbooks.
Classification: LCC TX715.2.S69 F79 2019 | DDC
    641.59/26872073—dc23 LC record available at
    https://lccn.loc.gov/2018032936

ISBN 978-0-525-57386-9
Ebook 978-0-525-57387-6

Printed in China

Book design by Laura Palese
Cover photography by Johnny Autry
Illustrations by Office of Brothers

10 9 8 7 6 5 4 3 2 1

First Edition

CONT

ENTS

ENCHILADAS Y TAMALES Y MÁS
(ENCHILADAS AND TAMALES AND MORE)   118

INTRODUCTION

TURN →

in Texas, it'd be easy to find yourself here: in a boisterous dining room, guided by a friendly hostess who leads you around a bevy of servers—all balancing oversize trays of sizzling platters and warning, "Hot plate! Hot plate!"—and past a matronly lady rolling flour tortillas as fast as her hands will allow.

The room is bright, its stucco walls adorned with vividly painted artwork and zigzags of brightly colored *papel picado*. A mariachi trio—clad in sequined black suits and most likely three tequila shots in—croons in the background. When you arrive at your table, a basket of warm, overly salted tortilla chips and a little dish of salsa awaits. As you settle in, you mindlessly swipe a few chips through the salsa and peruse the pliable, plastic-sheathed menu, but you don't need to look at it long. You already know the choices you need to make: Margarita with salt or without? Beef fajitas or chicken? Small queso or large? An extra enchilada à la carte?

This is the ubiquitous Tex-Mex restaurant, known to all Texans no matter where in the state they reside, be it in a large urban metropolis or a flyspeck town in the desert regions of the west. While I was growing up in Houston, this scene played out for me and my family time and again at Armandos and Felix Mexican Restaurant, our go-tos. My parents would take me and my sisters for a weeknight dinner, or for lunch on a Sunday after church. An order of queso always started the meal, and fajitas and enchiladas quickly followed.

To Texans, Tex-Mex food is a way of life. There are a vast number of cuisines to choose from when dining out during any given week, but Tex-Mex is more than just a meal you pick for a night. It's a style of food that's deeply woven into the cultural fabric. Family and friends enjoy some form of the cuisine frequently, both out at a neighborhood Tex-Mex joint or cooked up at home. It's certainly not the kind of food you look to for its health benefits—you won't find much that's redeeming about it in that department. Rather, it's what you look to for familiarity, comfort, a sense of home.

Since my early days in Houston, I've dedicated my life to cooking, working as a professional chef in Houston, Atlanta, Aspen, and on the West Coast for some thirty years. I've prepared extravagant meals for large events using classic French techniques; innovative and complex fare in high-end restaurants; homestyle Thanksgiving feasts for my extended family; small plates and bite-size samples for guests at myriad food festivals; and just plain ol' fat, beefy burgers on the backyard grill for friends. To me, cooking has the power to help people experience something that isn't just tasty, but also makes them feel satisfied, happy, and complete. I can think of a lot of cuisines that stir those feelings for me, but at the end of the day, it's Tex-Mex that makes me feel most at home.

I opened my first restaurant in Atlanta in 2007: JCT Kitchen, a Southern-inspired restaurant that's still serving seasonal dishes today. I proceeded to open a few more spots over the next handful of years, but the idea to bring a classic Tex-Mex joint to Atlanta kept tugging at me. Having settled in Atlanta and put down roots to raise a family, I needed the taste of home to truly feel as though the city were my own. In 2014 I had a chance to open The El Felix, a neighborhood Tex-Mex joint. It was good, but I wanted to dig deeper with Tex-Mex. So in

2015, I opened Superica, which is inspired by the rustic, low-key cantinas you find in Austin and West Texas. (In Spanish, *súper rica* means "super rich" or "super delicious.") I've been lucky to find a fellow Texas native, Kevin Maxey, who grew up in the Dallas–Fort Worth area, to help flesh out both restaurants, and together we've worked hard to share the best of what Tex-Mex is to us with all of Atlanta.

In my mind, there are three main "food groups" in the Tex-Mex playbook. First are the classics: tacos, nachos, tamales, enchiladas—all dishes found on the menus of the original Tex-Mex cafés that sprouted up in small Texas towns in the 1920s. Then there are the "Kings of Tex-Mex"—fajitas, the *parrilla mixta* (mixed grill), the frozen margarita—which were added to the fold in the 1970s by the likes of iconic restaurants like Ninfa's on Navigation in Houston and Joe T. Garcia's in Fort Worth. And last is a little something I call "Deeper into the Barrio": those dishes that are more traditionally Mexican in heritage but still common to the Tex-Mex scene: menudo, pozole, mole, ceviche, tacos *al pastor*.

Kevin and I set out to pay homage to all three groups on the Superica menu and to respect the traditions and recipes that have been part of Texas culture for more than a century. Thankfully, the endeavor has paid off. Within three years, we had opened a second location of The El Felix in Atlanta and three more Supericas, in Charlotte, North Carolina, and Houston, with more planned in the immediate future.

I love Tex-Mex—and not just because it was a regular part of my diet growing up. I love it for its rich simplicity. It doesn't require skill as much as it demands soul. It's neither pretentious nor overly complex. And while you can certainly dress it up, at its core, Tex-Mex is a cuisine for everyone. It's approachable, satisfying, and, when done right, just delicious.

Since opening The El Felix and Superica, I've noticed how people have made a real connection with this style of food. And I've come to realize that you don't have to be from Texas to absolutely love it. Bringing my version of Tex-Mex to Atlanta—and beyond—has taught me that it's something that should be shared with everyone, which, coincidentally, is how this humble cuisine came about in the first place: one culture sharing with another.

It seemed fitting to collect all my love for Tex-Mex and the recipes I've worked hard to develop and put them in a medium that would allow people to create it at home: a cookbook. I teamed up with food writer Jessica Dupuy, who has covered Texas cuisine for numerous publications over the past decade. Like me, she's a native Texan and a true Tex-Mex loyalist. Together, our goal was to write a book that would be a tribute to the cuisine's collective Native American, Mexican, and Texan heritage and to my endless pursuit of all things *súper rica*.

As a result, this book has a whole bunch of bits and bobs—knit together with lots of recipes—that I hope others find interesting. The history of this cuisine is rife with legends and yarns that have been spun for generations. Most every dish has some sort of tale behind it, and I've shared the ones that I find informative or entertaining. And the recipes, well, I had to share the best of everything! From breakfast to iconic entrées and the tradition of wood-fired grilling to desserts and adult beverages, everything is in these pages. It is all, to me, *súper rica*, and I'm thrilled to share it with new Tex-Mex fans and longtime devotees alike.

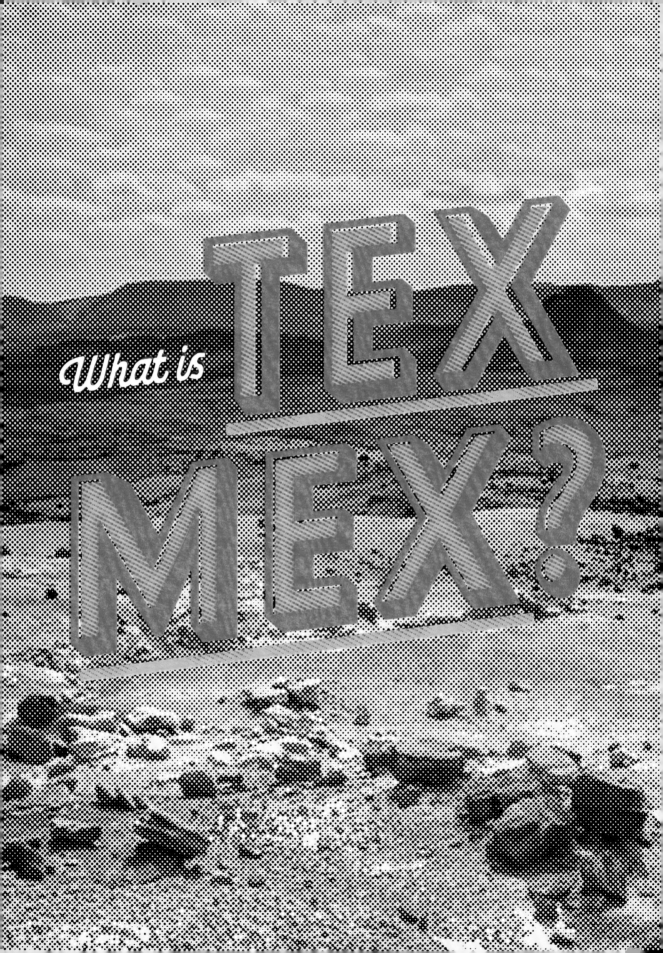

ONCE UPON A TIME, "Tex" and "Mex" were one and the same. Beginning in the sixteenth century, the territories now defined as Texas and Mexico were both a part of one large, ambiguous Spanish colony known as New Spain. The colony untethered itself from its mother country in 1821, and the First Mexican Empire was born. Fifteen years later, Texas fought for—and won—its independence from Mexico. But even though Texas would go on to join the United States of America in 1845, its identity—and therefore its foodways—had, by and large, already been forged by its deep roots in Mexico.

The first use of the term *Tex-Mex* had nothing to do with food, but rather came from the Texas-Mexican Railway, which was chartered in 1875 and quickly dubbed the "Tex-Mex Railway" by locals. In the early twentieth century, the term would come to refer to Tejanos, people of Mexican descent who had moved north into Texas. It was the culture Tejanos created that would most influence the evolution of Tex-Mex cuisine. Many of them found work as street vendors, selling food in San Antonio and southwest throughout the Rio Grande Valley, or in the kitchens of small-town diners and big-city restaurants as line cooks and dishwashers.

Bit by bit, enchiladas, crispy tacos, tamales, and chili con carne found their way onto menus as specials or permanent features. Though the cuisine was Mexican in nature, with ingredients such as corn tortillas, salsa, and chiles, it began to evolve as cooks used readily available American ingredients, which began to distinguish the cuisine as more Texan than strictly Mexican. Historical accounts of an eighteenth-century San Antonio–area settlement of Canary Island immigrants point to the introduction of cumin, a popular ingredient in North African cuisine, to Texas cooking culture. The Interstate Railroad brought flour from the eastern part of America to the corn-centric region of South Texas in the late 1800s, paving the way for flour tortillas to take a more central place on the table. In the early twentieth century, chili gravy, a true Tex-Mex creation that falls somewhere between a flour-based roux and a chile con carne sauce laced with cumin and chile powder, became a primary element, poured over enchiladas and tamales. Around the same time, the American industrialization period brought more shelf-stable processed cheeses, such as American cheese, that were not only cheaper but managed to melt beautifully into the chile-based sauces of Tex-Mex.

Throughout the twentieth century, items such as the Combo Plate—nachos, fajitas, and the revered bowl of chile con queso (or simply "queso")—began to have a regular place on restaurant tables in Texas. More and more "Mexican" establishments—icons such as Ninfa's on Navigation in Houston, Joe T. Garcia's in Fort Worth, La Fonda in San Antonio, Matt's El Rancho in Austin—began flooding the state in the 1970s and '80s. Though most of these places served food that seemed Mexican to American palates, there was really nothing authentically Mexican about them, a distinction the Mexican culinary maven Diana Kennedy brought to light when she panned

the stuff served north of the border as resolutely un-Mexican in her 1972 cookbook, *The Cuisines of Mexico*.

Years later, in 2004, famed food historian Robb Walsh pointed out that Tex-Mex has Kennedy to thank for drawing that line in the sand. It may have been that moment that allowed the cuisine to finally drop the now false identity of bastardized Mexican food and come into its own. In fact, Walsh referenced a 1973 article from the *Mexico City News* in which the term *Tex-Mex* was officially used to describe a cuisine completely separate from Mexican food. This break gave it permission to be its very own, beloved style of food— one that Texans would not only embrace with pride but also spread far and wide throughout the whole country as a definitively American cuisine. Interestingly, as the cooking style began to take hold around the country, a handful of Mexican American dishes from California and New Mexico were also lumped into the category. Things like burritos, fish tacos, and green chile stew aren't actually Tex-Mex at all—which is why you won't find specific recipes for any of them in this book. But unless you're in places south of San Diego or in Santa Fe, you're not likely to be corrected on these disparities.

To me, Tex-Mex is more than a checklist of menu items bound together by the flavors of chile, cumin, minced onion, and gooey, melted cheese. It is as much a look to the past and the cultures that laid the foundation for the cuisine as it is a look to the future, with regards to how it has spread throughout the country and the rest of the world. It owes both its origins and its broad expansion to the Mexican Americans who developed its definitive flavors and shared them in the kitchens of diners and restaurants across Texas and beyond. And for this Texan, who has now spent most of his adult life outside his native state, Tex-Mex and all its queso-gilded glory will always be a little piece of home.

Classic TEX-MEX BY THE MAP

MOST TEXANS DON'T CLAIM JUST ONE TEX-MEX RESTAURANT AS THEIR FAVORITE. Instead, they tend to designate preferences based on singular dishes. There's one place known for its queso, another for its enchiladas, another that's a must for fajitas. Depending on which part of Texas you're in, if you ask for a recommendation, folks might point you in a half-dozen directions. For example, my go-to spots in Houston have been Armandos and Felix Mexican Restaurant for queso and enchiladas, but I also love Ninfa's on Navigation and Little Pappasito's Cantina for fajitas, as well as Goode Company Taqueria for breakfast tacos.

Though there are many strong opinions held by many a Texan, the state has several inarguably iconic restaurants that deserve credit for bringing classic Tex-Mex dishes to fame in the first place. While the establishments listed here are just a few of the cuisine's pioneers, there are countless others that deserve just as much credit for championing the classics. Some of them, like Houston's Felix Mexican Restaurant (rest in peace), are no longer open, but many are indeed still serving up steaming combo plates all around the state. Here are some notables:

CASA RIO, in San Antonio, began serving up a traditional "Chili Queen" version of chile con carne in the 1940s.

Stacked enchiladas rose to fame with the help of the **OLD BORUNDA CAFE**, in Marfa, a favorite among West Texans from 1887 to 1987.

Since 1929, **MOLINA'S CANTINA** has been a Tex-Mex fixture in Houston as one of the first to serve cheese enchiladas using processed American cheese and chili gravy.

EL FENIX, in the Dallas–Fort Worth area, has served its famous "guacamole salad" since 1918.

Dallas's **EL CHICO'S CAFÉ** made pico de gallo a Tex-Mex standard with its *pico fría* (cold sauce).

Otis M. Farnsworth of San Antonio's **ORIGINAL MEXICAN RESTAURANT** introduced the idea of the combo plate, giving guests an easy way to enjoy a little bit of everything.

In Austin, **MATT'S EL RANCHO** introduced Bob Armstrong Dip (or *queso compuesto*), a steaming bowl of chile con queso served with scoops of taco meat, guacamole, and sour cream in the center. It's named for a former Texas legislator.

Houston's **NINFA'S** on Navigation is one of many restaurants—along with a local taco-shack cook Sonny Falcon of Kyle, a small town south of Austin, and Otilia Garza of Roundup Restaurant in Pharr, in the southernmost part of the state—that claim to have invented fajitas in the mid-1970s.

In San Antonio, it was **RAY'S DRIVE INN** that popularized the puffy taco in the 1950s.

TURN FOR MAP

CLASSIC TEX-MEX BY THE MAP

SAN ANTONIO

- La Margarita Mexican Restaurant and Oyster Bar
- Garcia's Mexican Food
- Soluna
- La Fonda on Main
- La Gloria
- Rosario's Mexican Restaurant & Lounge
- Mi Tierra Café y Panadería
- Casa Rio

HOUSTON

- Felix Mexican Restaurant (closed)
- Armandos
- Molina's Cantina
- Little Pappasito's Cantina
- The Original Ninfa's on Navigation
- Sylvia's Enchilada Kitchen
- Goode Company Taqueria

AUSTIN

- Curra's Grill
- El Méson
- Amaya's Taco Village
- Matt's El Rancho
- Polvos Mexican Restaurant
- Las Manitas
- Enchiladas y Mas

DALLAS

- El Fenix
- Cuquita's Restaurant
- Avila's Restaurant
- Café San Miguel (closed)
- Mariano's Hacienda

FORT WORTH

- Joe T. Garcia's
- Original Mexican Eats Cafe
- Uncle Julio's
- Salsa Fuego
- Esperanza's Restaurant & Bakery
- Lanny's Alta Cocina Mexicana (closed)

LAREDO

- El Meson de San Agustin
- Fonda Don Martin
- Palenque Grill

BROWNSVILLE

- Taqueria Rico's

EL PASO

- H&H Car Wash and Coffee Shop
- Forti's Mexican Elder Restaurant
- Tacos Santa Cecilia

MARFA

- Old Borunda Cafe (closed)

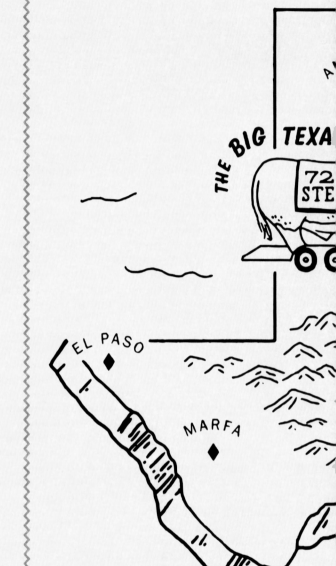

TOOLS

A kitchen stocked with basic utensils, pots, and pans is more than sufficient for Tex-Mex cooking. But this list also highlights some of the special, essential, or less common items that are worth seeking out if you plan to really take up Tex-Mex cuisine. I've explained how to use each piece of equipment here, though the recipes were written to use common tools to make it all more approachable and doable.

CAZUELA

These days, most beans and soups are cooked in a common soup pot on the stove. But back in the day, a clay *cazuela* was the more traditional piece of equipment for cooking and serving them. The pot works similarly to a Moroccan tagine, in that it conducts heat evenly. While you don't need one for cooking, they're excellent for serving beans and soups, or even as a punch bowl for sangria.

CHARCOAL GRILL

To be fair, there are pros and cons to cooking with both a charcoal grill and gas grill, but when it comes to cooking meat, especially for Tex-Mex cuisine, there's really no substitute for the charcoal variety. High heat is essential to get that special char on meat, and a charcoal grill can easily climb 100 to 200 degrees above the average gas grill. Moreover, it's the distinctive smoky flavor that a charcoal grill imparts that makes it a hands-down winner in the great grill debate every time.

CITRUS PRESS

You can always buy fresh or bottled juice from the market, but there's really no substitute for the extra-fresh flavor of citrus squeezed at home. Something changes as the juice sits in the shelf-stable bottles that isn't quite right. A citrus press is a simple tool that will make squeezing your own juices easier.

Comal

A *comal* is like a cast-iron skillet with very low sides. My first encounter with one was the sizzling-hot cast-iron tray on which fajitas were served, popping and spitting hot grease and juices from the grilled beef, onions, and peppers that sat on top. It wasn't until later that I found out how ubiquitous the *comal* is for properly heating tortillas, charring onions, and roasting peppers, tomatoes, or whole jalapeños for salsas. Whereas many Southerners might have a cast-iron skillet on their stovetop at all times, the *comal* is more commonly seen in kitchens throughout Texas, particularly in the southern and western parts of the state.

MOLCAJETE

The traditional tool for grinding spices and mixing chile pastes, the *molcajete* is nothing more than a mortar and pestle made of hand-carved lava rock, which has a much rougher surface than the materials used for standard mortars and pestles. It's also a really great tool for making and presenting guacamole.

TORTILLA PRESS

I've long extolled the virtues of handmade tortillas. Of course, today there are machines that handle mass production, but when you're making tortillas at home, there's nothing better than a good tortilla press to yield perfect rounds. Note that a press is specifically for making corn tortillas; it's better to roll out flour tortillas with a rolling pin. Be sure to press some wax paper or a cut-open plastic bag in between to keep the dough from sticking to the press.

TORTILLA WARMER

Almost as instrumental in delivering pliable, non-gummy tortillas as a *comal* is a tortilla warmer to keep them perfectly warm at the table. You can find fancy painted clay versions in Mexican markets, but the good ol' plastic and fiberglass ones work just as well. And if you can find the soft oven-mitt version, they're the best.

VAPORERA

If you're going to make tamales, you really need a good 20- to 30-quart *vaporera* or steamer with a steamer basket to get the job done right. Generations of families have used enameled cookware to make tamales, but you can find plenty of stainless-steel steam pots for a lot cheaper. Be sure it includes a steamer basket and lid.

Be it cheddar cheese, tortilla chips, and a jar of pickled jalapeños for a plate of nachos, or fresh tomato, onion, jalapeño, and a bunch of cilantro for a simple homemade salsa, these necessities are frequently at the ready. Most folks often have a few chili powders, some ground cumin, a box of three-alarm chili from a brand like McCormick, and a few cans of refried beans—pinto or black, depending on personal preference—around as well. But if you're starting from scratch, here's a comprehensive glossary for building the perfect pantry for Tex-Mex cooking.

Arroz

(Rice)—Next to beans, rice has long been one of the most important staples for Mexican American families throughout Texas. In South and West Texas ranches along the border, rice and beans alone could sustain a family in a time of scarcity. In Tex-Mex cuisine, they are a side to just about any order, and while too many restaurants treat them as an afterthought, I think it's worthwhile to make them memorable. I prefer to use a good-quality long-grain white rice like Mahatma brand.

CHICKEN BOUILLON

I don't use this ingredient a ton, but when it comes to Tex-Mex—both at home and in my restaurants—I let go of my "chefy" side and embrace chicken bouillon, as it's a perfect card to have up your sleeve for a punch of flavor. A little bit goes a long way for soups and sauces. My favorite is Caldo con Sabor de Pollo by Knorr.

CHILI POWDER

First, note that chili powder is not the same thing as *chile* powder. You can find a number of premade chili powders for chili con carne—there are even boxed kits with different powders that make you feel as if you're actually making the real thing. If you ask me, there's nothing wrong with them. Personally, I like mixing my own ingredients more deliberately, but it's okay to cut a few corners. I suggest using Gebhardt brand, as it delivers a true Tex-Mex flavor, in my opinion.

FRESH CILANTRO

This herb adds a bright little bite to salsas and tacos. I know it tends to be polarizing for people—you either love it or hate it. Personally, I think it's indispensable. But if you remain in the "hate it" group, try some Thai basil and/or fresh mint instead. It will take the dish in another direction, but you may like it.

CUMIN Though originally a Middle Eastern spice, cumin quickly found a home in Latin American cuisine. Like chiles and chili powder, it's one of the most distinguishing flavors of Tex-Mex food and is used in almost every cooked dish. It's always best to toast whole seeds and grind them yourself versus buying pre-ground.

Lard While lard has developed a bad reputation over the years, it's actually one of the healthier fats to cook with—but you have to be sure it's the real thing. The commercial lard you can buy at the store not only fails in delivering good flavor but is made of all sorts of processed chemical ingredients—it's truly not worth using. You can find the real thing at some butchers, but it's also super easy to make your own by rendering cubed pork fat trimmings at 250°F in a Dutch oven for a few hours. Stir occasionally during the cooking process and strain the lard into an airtight container once finished. It will last for up to a year in your fridge, or three years in the freezer. When you use the lard in things like refried beans and tortillas, the end result is no joke! Well worth the effort.

LEMON It's definitely more common to see limes used in Mexican food, but you'd be surprised at how often lemon gets used in Tex-Mex. Lemons have often been substituted for limes to bring a different vibrancy to guacamole and salsa. Though I'm more in the lime camp (as you'll see in my recipes), try substituting a little lemon, or even a blend of the two, and see what you like best.

LIME Most of the limes found in supermarkets are the larger Persian limes, but if you can get your hands on smaller Mexican limes (also called key limes), you should. In Florida, they're in peak season between June and August, but you can get the ones from Central and South America at grocery stores year-round. They're a little bit sweeter, very tart, and particularly delicious in Tex-Mex cuisine.

Masa (Fresh)—Fresh masa is a dough made with fresh soaked masa harina, and it's the best choice for making corn tortillas. It's a little hard to find, but some specialty Latin markets will have it. If you can find this dough premade, it puts you a step ahead of buying masa harina and making it yourself. (Note: You can also buy fresh masa made with lard, which is ready-to-go *tamal* dough.)

MASA HARINA A very soft flour made from finely ground hominy, dried corn kernels that have been cooked and soaked in lime water (a diluted solution of calcium hydroxide—not to be confused with water flavored with lime juice). The lime water is what gives corn tortillas and tamales their slightly sour flavor. Because the corn for masa harina has been treated with lime water, regular cornmeal cannot be used as a substitute. Masa harina can be found in many grocery stores or specialty markets.

MEXICAN CHOCOLATE This chocolate gets its distinctive flavor from the assortment of spices used to make it. Typical Mexican chocolate is made with roasted and ground cacao nibs, sugar, cinnamon, and sometimes nutmeg, allspice, nuts, and chiles. As a result, the chocolate can have a granular texture, but it's great to use in Mexican hot chocolate or as a dip for churros. You can find it pretty readily available at grocery stores or online.

MEXICAN OREGANO It's safe to say that not all oregano is created equal. The oregano species used for Greek and Italian food is not the same as what's used in Mexican food. Mexican oregano tends to be woodier and sweeter, giving Mexican recipes a distinctive flavor. You can buy it at most grocery stores in the dried spice section, and I recommend you do!

QUESO CHIHUAHUA

One of my go-tos for sure! This soft white-yellowish cheese similar to Monterey Jack and mozzarella is starting to appear in regular grocery stores in blocks or even grated. It originates in the Mexican state of Chihuahua, from which it gets its name. Interestingly, in Chihuahua it's called *queso menonita* after the Mennonite communities that first produced it. This cheese melts really well and is commonly used for queso fundido (see page 76). I love how stringy it gets when it's melted. But it does have a tendency to seize up, so dig in while it's hot.

QUESO OAXACA

This is a semihard white cheese that is close to those whole-milk (not fresh) mozzarella balls you can find in the grocery store. It has more of a string-cheese-like texture than soft fresh or buffalo mozzarella, and it works well as one of the cheeses in queso fundido (along with Chihuahua or Jack; see page 76) or chiles rellenos (see page 144). When searching for it at the market, look for long strands of string cheese rolled up into a softball-size ball.

QUESO VELVEETA

(or Processed American Cheese)—I don't have proof, but I imagine a lot of the cheese used in early Tex-Mex cooking was that neon-orange "government cheese" that used to be distributed to welfare and Social Security recipients. Processed Velveeta or Land O'Lakes Extra Melt still play a major role in old-school joints for chile con queso and cheese enchiladas. And, whatever your feelings are about it, you can't deny how beautifully it melts.

Rancho Gordo Beans

A lot of people argue that you really can't tell the difference between your standard commercial bulk beans and heritage beans, but I disagree. All you have to do is a little taste test to find out. California-based brand Rancho Gordo is one of the leading purveyors of heirloom beans in the country, and when you cook traditional Tex-Mex bean recipes with their beans, you'll understand why.

Tomato

When tomatoes are in season, I tend to use whatever kind is growing best in any given week. But generally, I stick to ones that are vine-ripened and big, like the beefsteak variety. For salsa in the dead of winter, I like to char them and cook them until they're fully softened through the middle, which helps intensify their flavor.

TOMATILLOS

A lot of people confuse tomatillos for green tomatoes, but in actuality, they aren't tomatoes at all. Originally from Mexico, they are wrapped in a papery husk and have a distinctive flavor that is both sweet and tart, making them great for salsas. When selecting them, make sure you stay away from ones with fruit that is dry and wrinkly. Stick with the plump, smooth ones. Remove the husks and rinse the fruit with water to remove any stickiness before using them.

TORTILLA

It's always a good idea to have tortillas on hand. Of course, making a homemade batch any time you need them isn't reasonable for everyday life, so when you have to buy tortillas, I suggest finding flour tortillas that are as fresh as possible. Some grocery stores—especially in Texas—make them fresh, but you can also look for a restaurant that makes them fresh and see if you can order some to go. For corn tortillas, yellow and white are both fine. For enchiladas, you want ones that are slightly dry and thin, as they tend to be more durable for baking in casserole form. Stick with the soft, fluffy ones for street-style tacos, for sure. The thicker ones can become too gummy.

TOTOPO

(Tortilla Chips)—Crisp little fried corn tortilla wedges are usually the first thing to greet you at a Tex-Mex table, along with a bowl of salsa. Depending on the restaurant or the brand, they range in thickness from hefty, with a crunch that splits the chip into shards of crumbs (great for queso), to thin, delicate, and pleasantly salty (great for fresh salsa).

A GLOSSARY OF CHILES

ANCHO
(DRIED POBLANO)

This large, wide, almost black, wrinkled chile is a dried poblano pepper that offers robust characteristics of raisins, pipe tobacco, and a hint of cocoa. It is one of the most common chiles used in making rich mole sauces (see page 107), a popular Oaxacan concoction often finished with a little Mexican dark chocolate.

CHILE DE ÁRBOL

These chiles are used for heat, but good heat! They tend to have an herbaceous and nutty flavor as well. Often called "bird's beak chiles," chiles de árbol are the primary component of our Super-Spicy "Staff Only" Salsa (page 116).

CHILE PEQUIN

Though originally named *chiltecpin* or *chiltepin*, an Aztec Nahuatl word meaning "flea chile," it's important not to underestimate the powerful bite this little chile can deliver. The chile pequin grows wild throughout Northern Mexico and South Texas. Many Texans keep a plant or two growing in their backyard to add a little perk to homemade salsas. Look for them at some farmers' markets, too. It's not uncommon to see dried pequins on tables throughout South Texas that some people can eat by the handful.

CHIPOTLE
DRIED & SMOKED JALAPEÑO PEPPER

This medium-size, shriveled-up chile is what you get when you smoke and dry a jalapeño pepper. These are found in most supermarkets in Texas and across the Southwest, but you can also get them canned in adobo sauce. Usually they are quite a bit hotter than the ancho chile (a dried poblano), and the two together make a great combination for sauces, soups like tortilla soup (see page 80) or pozole (see page 158), and salsas (see page 111).

GUAJILLO

Commonly used to blend with the sweetness of pasilla chiles when flavoring tamales, guajillo chiles are widely used throughout Mexico for their not-too-spicy, dynamic flavor and are frequently paired with chile de árbol for added heat. I learned that last tip from one of my cooks, Leticia, who used to always remind me, "Ford! Guajillo for flavor and árbol for heat!"

LONG GREEN CHILE

Most commonly found in West Texas, the term *long green chile* is often used interchangeably to refer to Anaheim, Chimayo, and Hatch chiles:

ANAHEIM CHILE A milder hybrid of the New Mexico green chile that is commonly roasted and served as a side dish or a garnish.

CHIMAYO CHILE A New Mexican long green chile named for the town of Chimayo, where the chiles are said to have the most dynamic flavor.

HATCH CHILE Another New Mexican long green chile named for Hatch, a town found in the southern part of the state. Hatch chiles are widely marketed when in season (during the summer) and often served roasted and skinned in sauces and salsas.

PASILLA

With characteristics of sweet raisin, pasilla chiles are commonly used to add flavor to sauces like mole (see page 107) and soups without adding too much heat.

JALAPEÑO

This plump green pepper is the most widely used—whether fresh or pickled—in American kitchens for adding spice to just about any dish. Jalapeños are prized for their herbaceous flavor and heat level, which can range from mild to hot depending on when they're harvested during the growing season (mid fall): the later in the season, the hotter the chile.

POBLANO

Larger and longer than other chiles, the poblano is very dark green in color and is the pepper most often used for stuffed chiles rellenos (see page 144) and *rajas con queso* (sliced poblano peppers and cheese).

SERRANO

The serrano pepper is one you'll often see Mexican and Texan cooks choosing over the jalapeño to make sauces and salsas because of the pepper's slightly more concentrated herbaceous flavors. Though smaller than a jalapeño, the serrano still packs quite a punch.

POBLANO

'OTLE

PEQUIN !

JALAPEÑO

SERRANO

PASILLA

SAN ANTONIO-STYLE
BREAKFAST SALSA   36

TROPICAL FRUIT SALAD
CON CHILE   39

MIGAS
40

CHILAQUILES
42

OX EYES
44

BREAKFAST TACOS 46

CAFE-STYLE PANCAKES WITH BUTTERMILK SYRUP   50

AGUAS FRESCAS
53

HORCHATA
54

OFTENTIMES, WHEN PEOPLE THINK OF THE quintessential TEX-MEX BREAKFAST,

they picture the breakfast taco. (Note: In Texas, we call them breakfast *tacos*, not breakfast burritos, which is a California thing.) But while the breakfast taco may be popular today, it's a relatively new phenomenon. In fact, I don't remember seeing it on menus until I was well into adulthood. The classic breakfast dishes—the ones served in restaurants and diners across the state of Texas—include *chilaquiles*, *migas*, and *huevos rancheros* or *divorciados*. These old-school Tex-Mex breakfast staples are a little more authentic to their Mexican heritage. And if you ask me, sitting down to a big plate of one of these beats an on-the-go breakfast taco any day. (Though I've never turned one of those down, either.)

SAN ANTONIO-STYLE
BREAKFAST
SALSA
PAGE 36

San Antonio–Style BREAKFAST SALSA

MAKES 2 CUPS

IN THIS STYLE OF SALSA, the tomato and chile flavors are particularly bright and flavorful. You typically see it served with breakfast at diners and Tex-Mex dives throughout Texas, particularly in San Antonio, hence the name. You'll almost always find it in a ceramic coffee creamer or one of those glass dispensers with a sliding lid that are typically reserved for syrup. It's the perfect accompaniment for Breakfast Tacos (page 46).

2 vine-ripened tomatoes

½ small onion, chopped

2 serrano peppers, stemmed

2 garlic cloves

1 teaspoon kosher salt, plus more as needed

¼ teaspoon ground cumin

1 In a medium saucepan over high heat, bring 1 quart water to a boil. Add the tomatoes, onion, serranos, and garlic and boil until the tomatoes are soft all the way through, about 7 minutes.

2 Drain the vegetables and transfer to a blender. Add the salt and cumin and purée until smooth. Taste and add more salt as needed.

3 Serve or store in an airtight container in the refrigerator for 2 to 3 days.

ATOLE,
FOR A SOULFUL BREAKFAST

Every culture has some form of warm breakfast cereal. Whether made from oats, rice, wheat, barley, or buckwheat, a local grain boiled down with water or milk is a foundational part of cuisines across the globe: In Asia there's congee and in Ethiopia ga'at. In Central and Eastern Europe they have kasha, while the Italians favor polenta. Most Americans are familiar with instant oats or creamy wheat porridge, and in the American South, grits are favored.

In Mexico, and north into the Rio Grande Valley of Texas, atole has long been a filling, inexpensive fixture at the breakfast table. With a base that's usually ground corn, this starchy cereal can also be made from a grain, including rice, oats, and even mesquite beans. The consistency falls somewhere between a thick porridge and a soupy smoothie. In fact, it's not uncommon for it to be consumed as a warm beverage in an earthenware mug rather than from a bowl with a spoon.

From as early as the fifteenth century, atole was a staple in times of poor hunting or harvest conditions among Mesoamerican and Texas's native peoples. Evidence of the cereal exists in the state as far back as the mid-sixteenth century, when Spanish explorer Cabeza de Vaca encountered the Coahuiltecan tribes of South Texas. After the corn was hand-ground with stone *molcajetes* (mortar and pestle), it was typically boiled with dried berries, prickly pear pulp, and herbs. Often, *piloncillo* (unrefined sugar) or wild honey was stirred in as a sweetener, a practice that is still common today. As Spanish exploration continued and cocoa began moving north, ground chocolate found its way into the dish, making for a markedly special treat known as *champurrado*.

While atole is still enjoyed today, it's a culinary treasure primarily celebrated among families and friends, particularly during the winter holiday season. While you may occasionally see it in small family-owned Tex-Mex cafés, it remains one of the best-kept secrets of Tex-Mex cuisine, served in home kitchens throughout South Texas and farther south into Mexico, particularly as a warm, comforting libation in the cold winter months.

TROPICAL FRUIT SALAD CON CHILE

SERVES 4

WE SERVE THIS SALAD as a side dish with brunch at Superica. Most people think they're getting a standard mix of fruit, but this version really gets a bit of a kick from the chile de árbol powder we sprinkle over it. The jicama and cucumber add a nice crunch, but the real magic comes from a freshly squeezed lime, a simple trick I learned from my dad. Serve it alongside Migas (page 40) or Chilaquiles (page 42).

4 cups cut fruit (any combination of watermelon, cantaloupe, mango, papaya, pineapple, orange, coconut, jicama, and cucumber; see Tip)

½ cup fresh lime juice

2 teaspoons kosher salt

2 teaspoons chile de árbol powder

2 radishes, thinly sliced

2 key limes, cut in half

1 tablespoon fresh cilantro leaves

1   Place the fruit in a large serving bowl and add the lime juice, salt, and chile powder. Toss to combine. Garnish with the radishes, lime halves, and cilantro. Serve immediately.

TIP I like to cut the fruit in different sizes, from 1- to 2-inch pieces, for a more interesting look and nice texture.

MIGAS

For centuries in Spain, and later in Mexico, *migas*—which means "crumbs"—were the leftover ingredients you'd find after a late-night celebration with family and friends, like a wedding or an anniversary party. The next morning, they would be repurposed into some sort of hearty, fortifying breakfast. In Tex-Mex cooking, the philosophy is similar: *Migas* are typically a scramble of eggs and variations of pico de gallo ingredients that are sprinkled with a bunch of day-old tortilla chip crumbs, likely from the bottom of the bag. This recipe includes a way to make your own tortilla chips, but you're welcome to use store-bought chips instead.

SERVES 4 TO 6

½ cup vegetable oil

8 (6-inch) corn tortillas, store-bought or homemade (page 98)

1½ teaspoons kosher salt

1 small onion, sliced

1 serrano pepper, stemmed and sliced

8 large eggs

1 cup grated Chihuahua or Monterey Jack cheese

½ small bunch cilantro

1 avocado, pitted, peeled, and sliced

TIP

The key here is not to stir the chips in too early while cooking the eggs, or they'll get too mushy and clumpy.

1 Pour the oil into a heavy medium pot and heat over medium-high heat to 350°F.

2 Stack the tortillas and cut them into 1-inch squares. Separate the pieces and carefully add them to the hot oil. Fry, stirring continuously, until light golden and crispy, 3 to 4 minutes. Using a slotted spoon, transfer the tortilla chips to a paper-towel-lined plate to drain. Immediately season with ¼ teaspoon of the salt.

3 Discard all but 2 tablespoons of the oil from the pot and return the pot to medium heat. Add the onion, serrano, and 1 teaspoon of the salt. Cook, stirring frequently, until the onion starts to soften, 2 to 3 minutes.

4 In a medium bowl, beat the eggs with the remaining ¼ teaspoon salt. Add the eggs to the pot and cook, stirring gently, until the eggs begin to set, 1 to 2 minutes. Add the tortilla chips, cheese, and cilantro and cook, stirring gently, until the eggs are just set, about 1 minute more.

5 Serve immediately with the avocado.

CHILAQUILES

Vegetable oil, for frying

10 (6-inch) corn tortillas, store-bought or homemade (page 98), cut into eighths

Kosher salt

2 cups roasted tomato salsa, store-bought or homemade (page 113)

¼ cup Standard Chile Paste (page 66)

1½ cups grated Oaxaca or mozzarella cheese

1 tablespoon unsalted butter

8 large eggs

Chilaquiles have long been in the canon of Mexican cuisine, with regional variations throughout the country. But this dish often gets confused with *migas*. Though they're both often served at breakfast or brunch, *chilaquiles* are more about the tomato salsa and chile paste that are paired with a crunchy tortilla and topped with a fried egg (or sometimes boiled meats), while for *migas*, you scramble the egg and tortilla bits together.

You can prepare the sauce a day or two in advance, but make sure it is warm before combining it with the tortilla strips. The key is to cook the *chilaquiles* as quickly as possible in the oven to keep the tortillas from becoming too mushy, and cold sauce slows the cooking time.

SERVES 4

1 Preheat the oven to 375°F.

2 Fill a large heavy pot with oil to a depth of 1½ inches. Heat the oil over medium-high heat to 350°F to 375°F.

3 Carefully add the tortilla pieces to the hot oil and fry, stirring frequently, until golden and crispy, 4 to 5 minutes. Using a slotted spoon, transfer the tortilla chips to a paper-towel-lined plate to drain. Immediately season with salt.

4 In a small saucepan set over medium heat, combine the salsa and chile paste. Heat, stirring occasionally, until boiling, 3 to 4 minutes. Transfer the sauce to a large bowl.

5 Add the chips and half the cheese to the bowl of sauce. Gently toss to combine and coat the chips. Transfer to a small baking dish and top with the remaining cheese. Bake until the chips are crispy and have deepened in color and the cheese has melted, 15 minutes.

6 Meanwhile, melt the butter in a medium sauté pan set over medium heat. Crack the eggs directly into the pan. Reduce the heat to low, cover, and cook until the whites are completely set but the yolks are still runny, 4 to 5 minutes.

7 Divide the baked chips among four serving plates. Top each with two eggs and serve immediately.

SERVES 4

HUEVOS DIVORCIADOS
con Chilaquiles

Huevos divorciados is a traditional Mexican breakfast that showcases the vibrantly different flavors of red salsa and green salsa. It is served as two fried eggs atop *chilaquiles* with a spoonful of red salsa over one egg and a spoonful of green over the other, hence their state of "divorce."

Chilaquiles
THIS PAGE

¼ cup roasted tomato salsa, store-bought or homemade (page 113), warmed

¼ cup salsa verde, store-bought or homemade (page 116), warmed

Divide the *chilaquiles* among four serving plates. For each serving, place 1 tablespoon roasted tomato salsa on one egg and 1 tablespoon salsa verde on the second. Serve immediately.

OX EYES

SERVES 4 TO 6

"OX EYES," OR "EGGS IN HELL," is a classic Tex-Mex brunch dish featuring poached eggs in a red chile sauce. It was popular with cattle ranchers in West Texas in the late 1800s, who could easily make the meal over the campfire using just one skillet.

Smoky Chile Sauce (recipe at right)
8 large eggs
8 tablespoons grated Chihuahua or Monterey Jack cheese
¼ cup chopped fresh cilantro
¼ cup finely chopped onion
1 avocado, pitted, peeled, and sliced

1 Place a rack in the center of the oven and preheat the oven to 375°F.

2 In a 10-inch cast-iron skillet set over medium-high heat, heat the sauce just until it boils, 5 to 6 minutes. Turn off the heat. Crack the eggs directly into the sauce, leaving a little space between each one. Top each egg with 1 tablespoon of the cheese. Carefully transfer the skillet to the oven.

3 Bake until the yolks are just set but still runny, about 10 minutes.

4 Garnish with the cilantro, onion, and avocado. Serve immediately, family-style.

SMOKY CHILE SAUCE

MAKES 2½ CUPS

1 (14-ounce) can whole peeled tomatoes
¼ cup lard (page 24)
2 thick slices heavily smoked bacon, cut in half crosswise
2 garlic cloves, smashed
1 small onion, chopped
1 cinnamon stick
Pinch of ground cloves
1 tablespoon kosher salt
½ cup chicken broth
⅓ cup Standard Chile Paste (page 66)

Pour the tomatoes and liquid from the can into a blender and purée.

Melt the lard in a medium saucepan set over medium-high heat. Add the bacon and cook, flipping occasionally, until browned, 3 to 4 minutes. Add the garlic and cook, stirring, until golden, about 30 seconds. Add the onion, cinnamon stick, cloves, and salt and stir to combine. Cook, stirring occasionally, until the onion is golden, 1 to 2 minutes. Add the tomatoes, broth, and chile paste and whisk to combine.

Reduce the heat to low and simmer until the sauce has reduced to 2½ cups, 10 to 15 minutes. Remove the cinnamon stick.

If not using immediately, store in an airtight container in the refrigerator for 2 to 3 days.

BREAKFAST TACOS

I'M NOT REALLY SURE WHEN breakfast tacos became the big deal they are today, but I remember first becoming aware of them when Goode Company Taqueria in Houston started serving breakfast in the '80s. The place was always packed; there was a line out the door every weekend. You would order the combination you wanted—anything from venison or jalapeño sausage to steak, bacon, chorizo, and more—and they would bring it out on a platter with beans, rice, and fresh flour tortillas so you could build your taco just the way you liked it.

One important tip: Don't overload your taco. Not only does it get messy if you do, but you'll miss out on the great flavor of the tortilla. When it comes to fillings, simple is best: bacon and egg, potato and egg, fajita and egg, chorizo and egg. I even like to wrap up *migas* (see page 40) as a breakfast taco.

CLASSIC BACON & EGG
Serves 4

8 slices bacon
8 large eggs
½ cup refried beans, store-bought or homemade (page 61)
½ cup grated Chihuahua cheese
8 (6-inch) flour tortillas, store-bought or homemade (page 101), warmed
1 cup San Antonio–Style Breakfast Salsa (page 36)
Kosher salt

1 In a large cast-iron skillet set over medium-high heat, cook the bacon until the fat renders and the bacon is crispy, 2 to 3 minutes. Using tongs, transfer the bacon to a paper-towel-lined plate to drain.

2 Carefully discard all but 1 tablespoon of the bacon fat from the skillet. Fry or scramble the eggs in the bacon fat to your desired doneness, working in batches as needed. Transfer to a plate and cover to keep warm.

3 To build each taco, place 1 tablespoon of the beans, 1 tablespoon of the cheese, 1 egg (or one-quarter of the eggs, if scrambled), and 1 slice of bacon on top of a warm tortilla. Top each with 2 tablespoons of salsa and a pinch of salt and serve immediately.

FAJITA & EGG
Serves 4

1 pound skirt steak
2/3 cup soy sauce
2/3 cup canned pineapple juice
3 garlic cloves, smashed
2 tablespoons vegetable oil
1/4 cup chopped onion
1 serrano pepper, chopped
1 teaspoon kosher salt, plus more as needed
8 large eggs
1/2 cup refried beans, store-bought or homemade (page 61)
1/2 cup shredded Chihuahua or Monterey Jack cheese
1 avocado, pitted, peeled, and thinly sliced
8 (6-inch) flour tortillas, store-bought or homemade (page 101), warmed
1 cup San Antonio–Style Breakfast Salsa (page 36)

1 Place the skirt steak in a large resealable plastic bag. Add the soy sauce, pineapple juice, and garlic, seal the bag, and turn to coat the meat. Marinate in the refrigerator overnight.

2 Remove the skirt steak from the bag and pat it dry (discard the marinade). Heat 1 tablespoon of the oil in a large cast-iron grill pan set over medium-high heat. When the oil shimmers, add the steak and cook for 1 minute on each side for medium-rare, or to your desired doneness. Transfer the steak to a cutting board and let it rest for 3 to 4 minutes. Slice it against the grain and then cut it into bite-size pieces.

3 Add the remaining 1 tablespoon oil to the grill pan and heat over medium-high heat. When the oil shimmers, add the onion, serrano, and 3/4 teaspoon of the salt. Cook, stirring continuously, until the onion is translucent, 1 to 2 minutes.

4 In a medium bowl, beat the eggs with the remaining 1/4 teaspoon salt. Pour the eggs into the pan with the onion. Cook, stirring continuously, until the eggs are just cooked through, 6 to 7 minutes.

5 To build each taco, place 1 tablespoon of the beans, 1 tablespoon of the cheese, one-eighth of the egg mixture, 1/4 cup of the steak pieces, and 1 or 2 slices of avocado on a warm tortilla. Top each with 2 tablespoons of salsa and serve immediately.

CHORIZO CON PAPAS
Serves 4

1 pound Yukon Gold potatoes
3/4 cup vegetable oil
Kosher salt
8 ounces Mexican (fresh) chorizo
1/4 cup chopped onion
1 serrano pepper, stemmed and chopped
8 large eggs
2 tablespoons chopped fresh cilantro
1/2 cup refried beans, store-bought or homemade (page 61)
1/2 cup grated Chihuahua cheese
8 (6-inch) flour tortillas, store-bought or homemade (page 101), warmed

1 Preheat the oven to 450°F.

2 Brush the whole potatoes with 1 tablespoon of the vegetable oil. Arrange them in a medium baking dish. Bake until you can easily pierce them with a small paring knife, about 1 hour. Remove the potatoes from the oven and let cool to room temperature. Cut the potatoes into 1/4-inch cubes.

3 Heat the remaining oil in a large cast-iron skillet set over medium-high heat. When the oil shimmers, add the potatoes in an even layer. Fry, without moving, until crispy brown on the bottoms, 5 to 6 minutes. Transfer the potatoes to a plate and season generously with salt.

4 Discard all but 1 teaspoon of the oil from the skillet and return the skillet to medium-high heat. Add the chorizo and cook, stirring occasionally, until browned, keeping it from crumbling too much, 2 to 3 minutes. Add the onion and serrano and cook, stirring frequently, until the onion is translucent, 1 to 2 minutes. Add the crispy potatoes and stir to combine.

5 In a medium bowl, beat the eggs with a healthy pinch of salt. Pour them into the skillet. Cook, stirring continuously, until the eggs are just cooked through, 6 to 7 minutes. Add the cilantro and stir to combine.

6 To build each taco, place 1 tablespoon of the beans, 1 tablespoon of the cheese, and one-eighth of the egg mixture on a warm tortilla. Serve immediately.

FAJITA
& EGG
PAGE 47

CHORIZO
CON PAPAS
PAGE 47

CLASSIC
BACON
& EGG
PAGE 46

CAFÉ-STYLE PANCAKES
WITH BUTTERMILK SYRUP

MAKES 10 TO 12 PANCAKES

WHEN DINING OUT for a Tex-Mex breakfast, I usually opt for something with eggs, but I love it when I see a menu that features a few "standard American" items as well, like house-made waffles or pancakes. If you ask me, there's nothing wrong with chasing down an order of *migas* with a few pancakes.

The best part of this recipe is the buttermilk syrup. The pancakes are really good, but it's the syrup that makes the meal.

1 cup all-purpose flour
1½ tablespoons sugar
1¾ teaspoons baking powder
½ teaspoon kosher salt
2 large eggs
1 cup whole milk
6 tablespoons unsalted butter, melted and cooled
Buttermilk Syrup (recipe at right), warmed

1   In a medium bowl, whisk together the flour, sugar, baking powder, and salt.

2   In a large bowl, beat the eggs until light yellow in color. Add the milk and melted butter and whisk to combine. Add the flour mixture and whisk just until combined (the batter should still have lumps).

3   Heat a large griddle or cast-iron skillet over medium heat. When the griddle is hot, using a ¼-cup measure, ladle the batter onto the griddle. Cook until bubbles begin to form around the edges and the pancakes begin to look dry, 3 to 4 minutes. Using a spatula, flip the pancakes and cook until golden brown on the second side, 2 to 3 minutes. Transfer to a plate and cover to keep warm. Repeat with the remaining batter.

4   Serve the pancakes with warm syrup on the side.

BUTTERMILK SYRUP

MAKES 1⅓ CUPS

1½ cups sugar
¾ cup (1½ sticks) unsalted butter
¾ cup whole buttermilk
1½ tablespoons light corn syrup
1½ teaspoons baking soda
1½ teaspoons vanilla extract
¾ teaspoon kosher salt

In a medium saucepan set over high heat, combine the sugar, butter, buttermilk, and corn syrup. Bring the mixture to a boil and cook, stirring continuously, until thickened slightly, 3 minutes. Remove the pan from the heat and stir in the baking soda. The mixture will bubble up. Add the vanilla and salt and stir to combine. Cover and set aside until ready to use, or let cool completely and store in an airtight container in the refrigerator for up to 2 weeks.

Just before serving, set the syrup over high heat and bring to a boil, whisking continuously. Remove from the heat and serve.

AGUAS FRESCAS

IN MY EARLY LIFE, I washed down most Tex-Mex meals with an ice-cold Coke. Sodas were usually the only nonalcoholic options on restaurant menus. In recent years, I've started to see *aguas frescas* more and more. These "fresh waters" are usually made with seasonal fruit and a little sugar, and many include flowers, seeds, and cereal grains (the popular rice-based horchata with cinnamon is particularly good—see page 54 for my recipe.) They're a fine alternative to alcoholic beverages at lunch or dinner, and they always make a great breakfast accompaniment. Here are three of my favorites.

MELON AGUA FRESCA

Serves 4

1 pound honeydew melon, peeled, seeded, and diced
3 tablespoons fresh lime juice, plus more to taste
2 tablespoons sugar
Ice, for serving
Lime slices, for garnish

1 In a blender, combine the melon, lime juice, sugar, and 1 cup water and purée until the mixture is smooth and the sugar has fully dissolved, about 45 seconds. Pour through a fine-mesh strainer set over a pitcher; discard the solids.

2 Add 1 cup water to the melon purée and stir well. Taste and add more lime juice as needed. Refrigerate for at least 1 hour and up to 1 day before serving.

3 Stir well and pour into glasses over ice. Garnish with lime slices and serve immediately.

AGUA DE JAMAICA

Serves 4

1 cup dried hibiscus flowers (*flor de Jamaica*; see Tip)
½ cup sugar
Ice, for serving

1 In a medium saucepan set over medium-high heat, combine the hibiscus flowers, sugar, and 4 cups water. Bring to a boil, stirring to dissolve the sugar. Remove the pan from the heat and let the syrup cool to room temperature.

2 Pour the syrup through a fine-mesh strainer set over a pitcher, pressing the flowers against the strainer with a wooden spoon to extract all the liquid; discard the solids. Refrigerate for at least 1 hour and up to 1 day before using.

3 Stir 4 cups water into the hibiscus syrup to dilute. Stir well and pour into glasses over ice. Serve.

Flor de Jamaica **can be found at some specialty markets or online.**

Horc

1 cup long-grain white rice

¼ cup whole unsalted raw
    almonds

1 cup sugar

1 teaspoon ground
    cinnamon

1 whole vanilla bean, split
    lengthwise and seeds
    scraped out

Ice, for serving

1 In a blender, combine the rice, almonds, and 5
cups water and purée until the almonds are finely
chopped, about 2 minutes. Refrigerate overnight.

2 Pour the mixture through a fine-mesh strainer
set over a pitcher; discard the solids. Add the
sugar, cinnamon, and vanilla seeds to the pitcher and
stir until the sugar has dissolved. Stir in 2 cups water.
Refrigerate for up to 7 days.

3 Pour into glasses over ice and serve.

**For a revamp of your typical
morning coffee, use horchata instead
of milk. Combine equal parts cold
coffee and horchata in a large glass
filled with ice.**

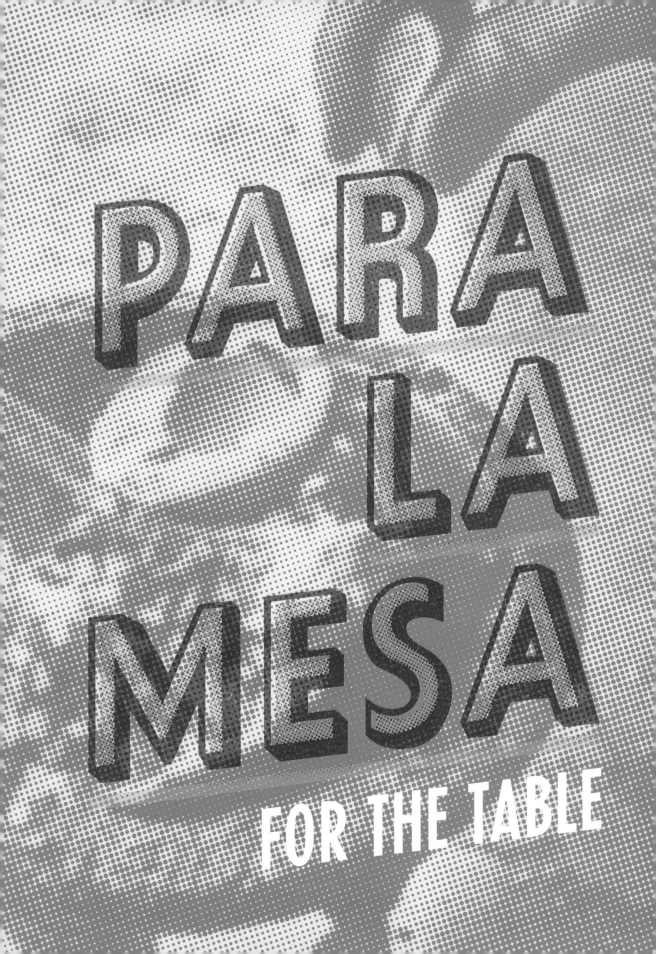

MEXICAN RICE AND REFRIED BEANS 60

PICKLED JALAPEÑOS 62

CHARRO BEANS 63

CHILE CON CARNE 65

GUACAMOLE
68

CHILE CON QUESO
72

"FELIX'S" QUESO
75

QUESO FUNDIDO CON CHORIZO 76

PUFFY TOSTADA CON QUESO 79

CHICKEN TORTILLA SOUP 80

ANY Good TEX-MEX MEAL

requires a lot of little details in order to be considered complete. A big part of the fun and deliciousness of these feasts is the myriad of side dishes and condiments that are passed around the table to share, bringing a nice communal feel to the experience.

Most people are sentimental, or at least highly opinionated, about the restaurants they believe have the freshest salsa, the creamiest queso, the smokiest tortilla soup, and the pork-iest refried beans—infused with the most lard! Not all Tex-Mex restaurants hit the mark on every one of them, which is why folks are particular about where to go for which favorite dish. The more time I've spent away from Texas, the more I've realized how important it is not to let any of these recipes be an afterthought. So I've spent a good amount of time cooking—and eating—different versions to come up with what I think are the very best of each.

REFRIED
BEANS
PAGE 61

MEXICAN RICE *and* REFRIED BEANS

ALMOST EVERY TEX-MEX DISH is served with a side of rice and beans—so much so that they're almost referred to as a single item. The rice is often cooked with a purée of fresh tomato, onion, and garlic, and sometimes laced with peas and carrots for a little flair. When served as part of a Tex-Mex combo plate (see page 123), the rice tends to be a little overcooked, and often the edges of the serving get a little crispy on the hot plate it shares with, say, a cheese enchilada. That unintentional yet glorious detail is a hallmark of Tex-Mex food, in my opinion.

Charro, a term for a Mexican cowboy, and black beans are modern additions to Tex-Mex menus. Prior to their debut, a serving of beans meant only one thing: soft pinto beans fried in lard and mashed into a flavorful, creamy concoction to be spread out into a velvety puddle on the hot plate alongside the rice. "Refried beans" is a bit of a misnomer. It actually refers to the Spanish term *frijoles refrito*, or "well-fried beans," which is certainly a more fitting description of the side dish.

MEXICAN RICE

Serves 4

1 teaspoon ground cumin

½ teaspoon kosher salt

1½ tablespoons tomato bouillon, such as Knorr

1 teaspoon chicken bouillon

1 tablespoon vegetable oil

1 cup long-grain white rice

1 large tomato, coarsely chopped

3 tablespoons finely chopped onion

3 tablespoons finely chopped carrot

1 tablespoon minced jalapeño pepper

1 tablespoon raw fresh or frozen corn kernels

1 whole jalapeño pepper, roasted and coarsely chopped

1 tablespoon roasted tomato salsa, store-bought or homemade (page 113)

1 In a medium saucepan set over high heat, combine the cumin, salt, tomato bouillon, chicken bouillon, and 1½ cups water. Bring the mixture just to a boil, stirring occasionally. Turn off the heat.

2 Heat the oil in a large saucepan set over medium heat. When the oil shimmers, add the rice and cook, stirring frequently, until it turns from opaque to brighter white, 2 to 3 minutes. Add the tomato, onion, carrot, minced jalapeño, and corn and cook, stirring frequently, until the onion is translucent, 3 to 4 minutes.

3 Add the bouillon mixture, roasted jalapeño, and salsa. Reduce the heat to medium-low and cook, stirring occasionally, until all the liquid has evaporated and small holes form in the surface of the rice, about 15 minutes. Cover the pan, remove from the heat, and set aside for 25 minutes to finish cooking in the residual heat.

4 Serve warm.

REFRIED BEANS

Serves 4

2 cups dried pinto beans (I like Rancho Gordo)

1½ cups finely chopped onion

1 tablespoon chili powder (I like Gebhardt)

1 teaspoon ground cumin

1 teaspoon kosher salt

1 teaspoon freshly ground black pepper

½ cup lard (page 24)

1 cup shredded cheddar cheese

1 Place the beans in a large pot and cover with water by 2 inches. Bring the water to a simmer over medium-high heat. Reduce the heat to low, then add the onion. Simmer, stirring occasionally, until the beans are tender, about 3 hours, adding more water as needed to keep the beans covered.

2 Ladle enough liquid from the pot into a bowl so the water level is just below the top of the beans; set the water in the bowl aside. Add the chili powder, cumin, salt, and pepper to the pot and stir to combine. Using an immersion blender, purée the mixture until smooth (alternatively, mash it with a potato masher).

3 Melt the lard in a large saucepan set over medium-high heat. When the lard shimmers, add the puréed beans and whisk to incorporate the lard. Bring the mixture to a boil, stirring occasionally, 3 to 4 minutes. Taste and add more salt as needed. Add the reserved cooking liquid to the beans as needed, ¼ cup at a time, to obtain a creamy consistency.

4 Sprinkle individual servings with ¼ cup shredded cheddar cheese and let melt. Serve warm.

PICKLED JALAPEÑOS

MAKES 1 QUART →

¼ cup canola oil

1 cup sliced onion

1 cup thinly sliced carrots

1½ cups white vinegar

1 tablespoon dried Mexican oregano

1 bay leaf

1 whole clove

2 teaspoons kosher salt

2 cups thinly sliced jalapeño pepper rounds

A COMMON DARE among Tex-Mex fans is to see who can eat a whole pickled jalapeño pepper without crying. I think that challenge helped me lay a foundation for tolerating spicier foods, but it was no easy task—though thankfully we always chased them with an ice-cold beer. There are so many versions of this ubiquitous recipe, and mine is to pickle the peppers with onion, slices of carrot, and sometimes even cauliflower. The vegetables take on the heat from the jalapeño, and they add a nice bite to just about anything you're eating, from nachos to tacos to queso and chips, or they're great served simply in a snack bowl on their own. Just don't forget that cold beer.

1 Heat the oil in a medium saucepan set over medium heat. When the oil shimmers, add the onion and carrot and cook, stirring, until the carrots are tender, 7 to 10 minutes. Add the vinegar, oregano, bay leaf, clove, and salt. Increase the heat to high and bring the mixture to a boil, stirring occasionally. Reduce the heat to low and simmer until the flavors have combined, about 5 minutes. Remove the pan from the heat, add the jalapeño rounds, and set aside to cool to room temperature, about 2 hours.

2 Pour the jalapeño rounds and liquid into a 1-quart glass jar with a lid and refrigerate for about 4 hours before the first use.

3 The pickled jalapeños will keep in the refrigerator for up to 1 month.

Charro BEANS

MAKES 4 CUPS

I LIKE TO CALL THESE "soupy beans," mainly because that's what they were called by the ladies who brought them to the table at the Mexican restaurants we frequented when I was a kid. Considering the beans always arrived in a little bowl as whole pinto beans cooked down in broth with bacon, onion, cilantro, jalapeño, and a few other seasonings, I believe they were aptly named. Sometimes you'll find *borracho* (drunk) beans on Tex-Mex menus, which simply means beer was included in their broth. Either version could truly be a meal unto itself, and some Tex-Mex restaurants will even offer them as a soup option.

8 ounces dried pinto beans

2 ounces bacon (about 2 slices), coarsely chopped

½ cup chopped onion

½ cup chopped tomato

1 small jalapeño pepper, stemmed and sliced

2 garlic cloves

½ cup packed fresh cilantro leaves

¼ cup chili powder (I like Gebhardt)

1½ teaspoons kosher salt, plus more as needed

Place the beans, bacon, onion, tomato, jalapeño, garlic, cilantro, chili powder, and salt in a large pot and cover with water by 1 inch. Bring to a simmer over high heat. Reduce the heat to low, cover, and simmer, stirring occasionally, until the beans are tender, 45 minutes to 1 hour, adding more water as needed to keep the beans covered. Taste and add more salt as needed.

chile con carne

THERE WAS ONCE A COOK at the River Oaks Country Club in Houston named Larry who used to make amazing chili. Larry's Screaming Eagle Chili. I convinced him to give me the recipe on the condition that I wouldn't ever share it. And I haven't, though I have to admit that I still use bits and pieces of it, with tweaks here and there, so I'm not technically breaking my promise. But he should get credit for getting me started.

The first big choice to make when cooking chili is the type of meat you'll use. Some people prefer small chunks of stew meat or, if they're feeling indulgent, small cubes of beef short rib, while others prefer "chili grind," or coarse-ground, meat. I personally like the latter, since I think it absorbs more flavor, and the meat and chiles become more unified.

The one thing I'm pretty adamant about is that beans have *no* place in a bowl of chili. I never even saw such an atrocity until I worked in Colorado. Beans seem like unnecessary filler that leave less room for meat!

4 slices thick-cut bacon, finely chopped

Vegetable oil

2 pounds coarse-ground beef chuck

1 medium onion, chopped

3 garlic cloves, coarsely chopped

2 jalapeño peppers, stemmed and chopped

2 teaspoons kosher salt

¼ cup chili powder (I like Gebhardt)

2 teaspoons ground cumin

2 cups beef broth

½ cup Standard Chile Paste (recipe follows on page 66)

2 cups corn chips, for serving

1 cup sour cream, for serving

1 cup pico de gallo, store-bought or homemade (page 112), for serving

½ cup chopped fresh cilantro, for serving

1 In a large heavy pot set over medium-high heat, cook the bacon, stirring frequently, until it is brown and crispy and the fat has rendered, 7 to 8 minutes. Using a slotted spoon, transfer the bacon to a paper-towel-lined plate to drain; reserve the fat in the pan. If needed, add oil; you want 3 tablespoons total fat in the pan.

2 Heat the bacon fat over high heat. When it shimmers, add the ground chuck and cook, stirring and breaking up the meat with the back of a wooden spoon, until well browned, 4 to 5 minutes. Add the onion, garlic, and jalapeños and cook for 3 to 4 minutes until the vegetables are softened. Return the bacon to the pan and stir to combine. Add the salt, chili powder, and cumin and cook until the spices are fragrant, about 1 minute. Add the broth and bring to a boil, stirring occasionally. Reduce the heat to low and stir in the chile paste. Cover and simmer until the meat is tender and soft, 2 hours.

3 Serve the chili with corn chips, sour cream, pico de gallo, and cilantro.

TIP Don't be afraid to use store-bought chili powders, though look for good ones like Gebhardt and Mexene brand.

STANDARD CHILE PASTE

MAKES ABOUT 2 CUPS

1 cup vegetable oil

3 ounces dried guajillo chiles (about 20), stemmed

1 ounce dried chiles de árbol (about 35), stemmed

4 garlic cloves

2 teaspoons kosher salt

1 teaspoon chicken bouillon

Heat the oil in a heavy medium pot set over medium-high heat. When it shimmers, add the guajillos, chiles de árbol, and garlic and cook, stirring frequently, until the chiles turn slightly darker in color, 30 to 40 seconds.

Carefully discard the oil from the pot, then carefully add water to just cover the chiles. Return the pot to high heat, cover, and bring the water to a boil. Cook until the chiles have softened, 5 to 7 minutes.

Drain the chiles in a strainer set over a bowl; reserve the soaking liquid. Transfer the chiles to a blender and add 1 cup of the reserved liquid, the salt, and the bouillon. Purée until smooth, stopping occasionally to scrape down the sides of the blender jar, 1 to 2 minutes.

The chile paste will keep in an airtight container in the refrigerator for up to 2 weeks.

CHILI:
A LONG-SIMMERED HISTORY

Fun fact: Chili has been the official state dish of Texas since 1977. But its origins predate this honorary distinction by hundreds of years, as it has roots in *chile con carne*, which existed long before Spanish colonization of the Americas in the seventeenth century.

Some say chili migrated from Mexico to San Antonio only as far back as the early 1800s and was served as a common local dish. There are many accounts from city journals and newspapers referring to a spicy beef *caldo* (soup) that was served by street vendors and in neighborhood diners. During that time, it took on the more anglicized name "chili," exchanging an *i* for the *e* at the end of the word.

Other accounts show that chili dates even further back, to the eighteenth century. It's been documented that native tribes in West Texas and throughout the Chihuahuan Desert would make a dried chile paste to use as a preservative and antiseptic for meat while traveling on the open plains. At some point, the dish was picked up by Spanish missionaries, and then European settlers and ranchers discovered it later on from the missions as they moved cattle across the state throughout the 1800s.

By the 1860s, chili was a street-vendor staple at San Antonio's Military Plaza, where families would set up booths each night and sell chili out of large stockpots. Mothers and daughters would dress in colorful costumes to lure more customers to their tables, and these brightly clad beauties were given the name Chili Queens. These women carried on the tradition through the 1930s.

In the 1880s the Interstate Railroad brought visitors from the outside world to Texas and introduced them to its spicy fare. In 1893, the San Antonio Chili Stand was set up at the Chicago World's Fair, and by the 1920s, chili was being canned and sold in Oklahoma, Missouri, and Ohio.

Modern-day chili is still commonly served as a meal unto itself, garnished with shredded cheese and minced white onion, but it has also become a garnish to hot dogs sold in ballparks and is found sold in combination with corn chips as the popular football stadium and state fair mainstay "Frito pie."

Regardless of how you choose to simmer your batch, chili remains a hearty, delicious dish that can both comfort and sustain many.

GUACAMOLE

AVOCADOS ARE THE STAR HERE, which means you have to pick good ones. No amount of salt or lime juice will be able to mask a yucky avocado. The fruit should be fairly firm when gently squeezed, with just a little bit of give to indicate perfect ripeness. Also, I find that a good sea salt, like Maldon, makes a big difference in the taste and texture of the guac. In terms of consistency, I like my guacamole somewhere between really creamy and a bit chunky, so that you sometimes get a little bite of straight avocado. And a word of warning: Never make guacamole ahead of time. It will oxidize and become brown. Always serve it immediately after you've mixed it together.

4 avocados, pitted and peeled

1½ tablespoons fresh lime juice

½ cup finely chopped onion

¼ cup finely chopped fresh cilantro

2 tablespoons finely chopped jalapeño pepper

½ teaspoon kosher salt or sea salt, plus more as needed

In a medium bowl, mash the avocados with the back of a large spoon. Add the lime juice, onion, cilantro, jalapeño, and salt. Using a rubber spatula, fold to combine. Taste and add more salt as needed. Serve immediately.

GUACAMOLE:
IT'S MORE THAN A DIP

The word *guacamole* stems from the Aztec Nahuatl words *ahuacatl* (avocado) and *molli* (mixture), suggesting that its origin may predate the thirteenth century, which was the height of the Aztec empire. In pre-Columbian Mexico, guacamole was likely a mash of avocado with wild onion, chile, and maybe tomato or tomatillo. Cilantro and limes wouldn't join the fold until after the arrival of the Spanish, who brought them to the New World.

In recent years, guacamole's popularity at the Tex-Mex table—and many other tables, for that matter—has skyrocketed. (According to the Hass Avocado Board, sales of avocados doubled between 2005 and 2015.) Loosened import restrictions, as well as a growing Hispanic population from Central America, where the majority of avocados are grown, have contributed to the influx of the creamy green fruit. Not to mention the influence of headlines about the health benefits of avocados—people think they're doing something good for themselves by eating plenty of guac. But personally, I think any health boost is merely a bonus, because avocados are just plain delicious.

When it comes to authentic Mexican guacamole, lime—or lemon—is typically avoided. Cookbooks, including Diana Kennedy's *The Art of Mexican Cooking* and *Hugo Ortega's Street Food of Mexico*, suggest that the addition of the vibrant acidity disrupts the balance of the avocado flavor in guacamole. But in Tex-Mex cooking, you'll see both lime and lemon used, though lime is more common. I have to admit, there's something familiar and distinctive about a citrus punch in Tex-Mex guacamole. I like to alternate between the two depending on my mood, but I always use them sparingly.

CHILE
con
QUESO

To me, there are really two kinds of "classic" chile con queso. First, there's the two-ingredient version, in which one block of Velveeta is melted and one can of Ro-Tel diced tomatoes with green chiles is stirred into the melted cheese. The second is a more chef-driven method that combines a creamy Mornay sauce of milk, flour, and cheese with chiles. I'm a fan of both styles equally. That's right—this chef *loves* processed cheese! But it needs milk or stock to thin it out. I like to borrow from both of these classics, using 75 percent processed cheese and 25 percent Chihuahua cheese blended together with milk lightly thickened with a roux. (I use cornstarch to keep the roux gluten-free.)

MAKES 2 CUPS

1 tablespoon vegetable oil

¼ cup chopped onion

¼ cup chopped poblano pepper

1 tablespoon chopped jalapeño pepper

¼ cup roasted tomato salsa, store-bought or homemade (page 113)

¼ cup half-and-half

1 tablespoon cornstarch

¾ teaspoon ground cumin

¾ teaspoon garlic powder

½ teaspoon kosher salt, plus more to taste

6 ounces Velveeta cheese, grated

2 ounces Chihuahua cheese, grated

Corn tortilla chips, for serving

1 Heat the oil in a large saucepan set over medium heat. When the oil shimmers, add the onion, poblano, and jalapeño and cook, stirring continuously, until the onion is translucent, 3 to 4 minutes. Add the salsa and cook, stirring frequently, until all the liquid has evaporated and the mixture is dry, 5 to 10 minutes.

2 In a small bowl, whisk together the half-and-half, cornstarch, cumin, garlic powder, and salt. Add the mixture to the saucepan along with ⅔ cup water. Whisk to combine. Bring to a simmer, whisking frequently. Add the cheeses, a little at a time, stirring as they melt to combine. Return the mixture to a simmer and cook, stirring frequently, until all the cheese has melted completely, 2 to 3 minutes.

3 Serve immediately with tortilla chips.

EL QUESO?

By definition, *chile con queso*—or "queso," as it's most commonly known—simply means "cheese with chile." But for those who have developed an unshakable love for this tasty dip (which is pretty much anyone who's ever tried it), queso is as much a part of our identity as it is a beloved appetizer.

Early references to this gooey dip date back to the 1800s, when it made appearances in Mexican literature (*El Periquillo Sarniento* by José Joaquín Fernández de Lizardi) and cookbooks (*La Cocinera Poblana*). In the 1900s, a similar concoction called Mexican rarebit, after Welsh rarebit, a savory cheese sauce, popped up in Kentucky, California, and Massachusetts newspapers. But the queso we know and love today first appeared in recipe form in a 1920s cookbook by the Woman's Club of San Antonio, after which it became a fairly common side dish.

In 1916, a processed cheese made from a mixture of Colby and cheddar, with curds and emulsifiers, was created by the Kraft food company. During World War II, this "American cheese" was used in military kitchens. Following the war, as a way to maintain the price of dairy when industry subsidies led to a surplus of milk, the government made a whole bunch of American cheese, which was given to welfare beneficiaries. This processed cheese was made more popular in the mass market by Kraft, who created single-serving slices of American cheese and an easy-melting cheese product called Velveeta.

Queso got its big break as a Tex-Mex classic in the 1940s, when the Texas-based Ro-Tel company began to market its recipe for stirring their canned tomatoes with green chiles into melted Velveeta as a dip to be served with tortilla chips. The rest, as they say, is history. Each of the quesos I've shared in this book is a classic in its own way.

"FELIX'S" *queso*

MAKES 2 CUPS

3 dried chiles de árbol, stemmed

1 cup boiling water

½ cup vegetable oil

1 cup drained canned diced tomatoes

½ cup finely chopped onion

2 garlic cloves, minced

1½ teaspoons sugar

½ teaspoon ground cumin

½ teaspoon kosher salt

¼ teaspoon freshly ground black pepper

2 tablespoons all-purpose flour

2 cups grated yellow American cheese

Corn tortilla chips, for serving

OPENED IN 1937 BY FELIX TIJERINA and his family, Felix Mexican Restaurant was one of Houston's iconic Tex-Mex joints, serving generations of Houstonians until its closing in 2008. Tijerina made an indelible mark on the city in his own right as a community activist pioneering an English-immersion program, the Little Schools of 400, for Hispanic first-grade students, which became the inspiration for Lyndon B. Johnson's Head Start program, one of the country's most successful federal initiatives. The restaurant's queso was famous, arriving at the table in a small bowl rimmed with reddish oil from the sautéed vegetables that had been stirred into the cheese. It was a thicker style of queso that hung onto the chip, and it was different from any other I've ever had.

I've done my best to re-create Felix's amazing queso based on a clipping about it from an old *Houston Chronicle* article. A word of warning: If you didn't grow up on this dish, you might say, "Ford??!?!? What are you thinking?!" Just trust me.

1 Put the chiles in a small bowl and pour over the boiling water. Let sit for 5 minutes to soften the chiles. Drain and chop the chiles.

2 In a medium nonstick skillet over low heat, combine the chopped chiles, oil, tomatoes, onion, garlic, sugar, cumin, salt, and pepper. Cook, stirring frequently, until the onion and chiles have softened, 10 to 15 minutes.

3 In a small bowl, stir together the flour and 2 tablespoons water to make a paste. Add the paste to the skillet and cook, stirring until the mixture is well combined, for 2 minutes. Add the cheese and cook, stirring continuously, until the cheese has melted, 3 to 4 minutes.

4 Serve immediately with tortilla chips.

QUESO FUNDIDO CON CHORIZO

MAKES 2 CUPS

QUESO FUNDIDO means "molten cheese," and you'll sometimes find this dish listed on menus as *queso flameado*, or "flamed cheese." It's essentially broiled white cheese that gets its name from literally being on fire in a cast-iron dish. Usually you'll see it cooked with chorizo, shrimp, mushrooms, or poblano peppers. I love its stringy quality and how it expands as you pull it away from the dish. I'm pretty sure some recipes use mozzarella cheese, which is a good option for that stretchy effect, but I like Oaxaca and Monterey Jack cheeses for their flavor. This dish is best served with flour tortillas.

6 ounces Mexican (fresh) chorizo, crumbled

8 ounces Chihuahua cheese, shredded

4 ounces Monterey Jack cheese, shredded

4 ounces Oaxaca cheese, shredded

1 teaspoon dried Mexican oregano

6-inch flour or corn tortillas, store-bought or homemade (page 101 or 98), for serving

1 Place a rack 6 to 8 inches from the heat source and preheat the oven to broil.

2 In a medium sauté pan set over medium heat, cook the chorizo, stirring, until lightly browned and cooked through, 5 to 6 minutes. Using a slotted spoon, transfer the chorizo to a paper-towel-lined plate to drain.

3 In a medium bowl, combine the chorizo, all the cheeses, and the oregano and toss to combine. Transfer the mixture to a shallow ovenproof baking dish.

4 Broil until the cheese is bubbling and golden brown on top, 4 to 5 minutes.

5 Serve immediately, dolloping a spoonful or two onto the center of a warm tortilla and rolling it up like a taco.

PUFFY TOSTADA CON QUESO

SERVES 4

YOU DON'T SEE THIS DISH on Tex-Mex menus very often these days, but those who remember that crispy puff of fried corn tortilla doused with creamy chile con queso know it was a thing of legend. They might be part of a combo platter listed on the menu as "Cheese enchilada, crispy beef taco, and chile con queso," but the queso would come out on a separate plate, poured on top of a crisp, puffed shell. I liked to crack it open with my fork to watch the steam come out. Though it seemed proper to eat it with a fork and knife, you really only needed a utensil to crack it—after that, you had to just get in there with your fingers.

Vegetable oil

12 (6-inch) corn tortillas, store-bought or homemade (page 98)

2 cups Chile con Queso (page 72)

½ cup finely chopped onion

¼ cup chopped fresh cilantro

1 Fill a deep, heavy pot or Dutch oven with oil to a depth of 1½ inches. Heat the oil over medium-high heat to 375°F. Line a wire rack with paper towels, place it on a baking sheet, and set it nearby.

2 Working one at a time, carefully place a tortilla in the hot oil. Fry the tortilla, continuously spooning oil over the top with a large metal spoon, until it begins to puff, 10 to 15 seconds. Continue to baste the tortilla and cook until golden brown, 1 minute. (Do not flip the tortilla.) Using a slotted spoon, transfer the tortilla to the prepared rack to drain. Repeat with the remaining tortillas, letting the oil return to 375°F after frying each one.

3 When ready to serve, gently push down on the tops of the puffed shells to create small openings. Place a generous spoonful of queso into each tostada. Top each with 2 teaspoons of the onion and a sprinkling of cilantro. Serve immediately.

chicken

FOR THE TORTILLA STRIPS

8 (6-inch) corn tortillas, store-bought or homemade (page 98)

Vegetable oil, for frying

Kosher salt

FOR THE BROTH

1½ quarts chicken broth

1 small onion, quartered

1 carrot, coarsely chopped

1 celery stalk, coarsely chopped

1 poblano pepper, seeded and coarsely chopped

¼ cup chopped fresh cilantro

½ teaspoon dried Mexican oregano

2 (6-inch) corn tortillas, store-bought or homemade (page 98)

1½ teaspoons kosher salt, plus more to taste

Tortilla soup is a Mexican classic that has earned an enduring place in Tex-Mex cuisine. Traditionally made with a base of tomato and chicken broth, the soup is often laced with aromatic epazote in Mexico, but in Tex-Mex you see cilantro used more often as the flavoring agent. Dried chiles add a depth of flavor that makes the soup even more delicious. And, of course, freshly fried strips of corn tortillas are this dish's signature. Serve them on top of the soup with a few slices of avocado, mesquite-grilled chicken fajita meat, and a sprinkle of Monterey Jack or queso fresco, and you've turned the humble chicken soup into a special meal.

1 MAKE THE TORTILLA STRIPS Fill a Dutch oven or other heavy pot with oil to a depth of 1 inch. Heat the oil over medium-high heat to 350°F. Line a wire rack with paper towels, place it on a baking sheet, and set it nearby.

2 Cut the tortillas into thin strips, about ¼ inch wide. Carefully add a few tortilla pieces at a time to the hot oil and fry them, stirring gently, until golden and crispy, 2 to 3 minutes. Using a slotted spoon or tongs, transfer the strips to the prepared rack and lightly season them with salt. Repeat with the remaining tortilla pieces. Carefully discard the oil.

tortilla soup

FOR THE SOUP

1 (15-ounce) can hominy, drained and rinsed

1 small onion, sliced

2 small carrots, sliced

1 small zucchini, sliced

2 cups coarsely chopped Fajita Chicken (page 188) or store-bought rotisserie chicken

1 cup shredded Chihuahua cheese

1 avocado, pitted, peeled, and diced

½ cup pico de gallo, store-bought or homemade (page 112)

3 MAKE THE BROTH In the same Dutch oven, combine the broth, onion, carrot, celery, poblano, cilantro, oregano, and salt. Bring to a simmer over medium heat, stirring occasionally. Reduce the heat to low, cover, and simmer, stirring occasionally, until the vegetables have softened, 1 hour. Strain the broth, discarding the solids. Taste and add more salt as needed. Return the broth to the pot and set the pot over low heat.

4 MAKE THE SOUP Add the hominy, onion, carrots, and zucchini to the broth. Increase the heat to high and bring to a boil, stirring occasionally, about 10 minutes. Add the chicken and bring the soup back to a boil.

5 Divide the soup among four serving bowls. Garnish with the cheese, avocado, pico de gallo, and tortilla strips and serve.

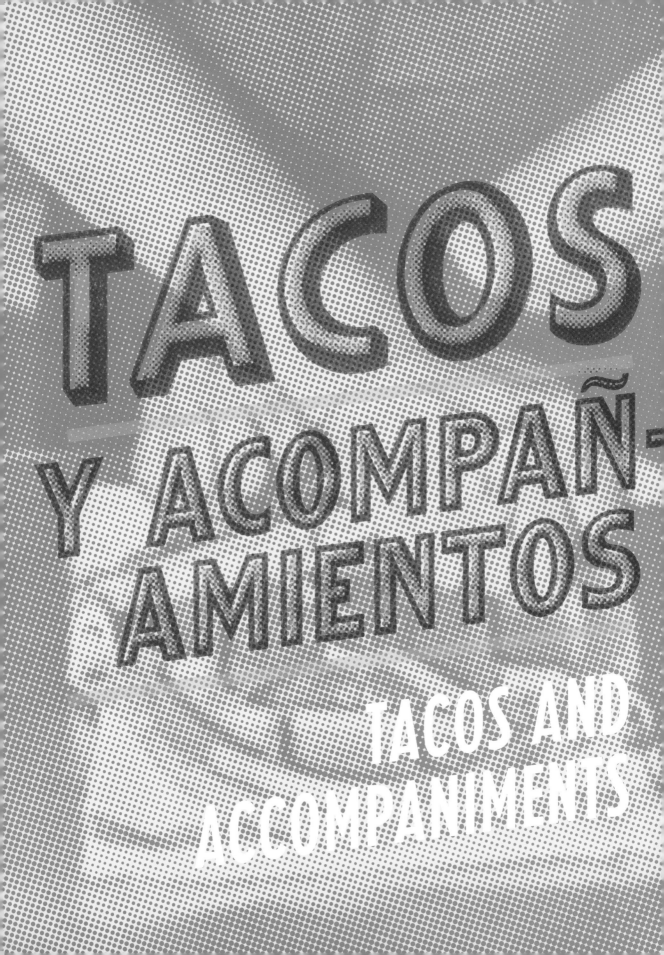

CRISPY TACO SHELLS 97

CORN TORTILLAS 98

PUFFY TACO SHELLS 98

FLOUR TORTILLAS 101

BEEF PICADILLO 103

BRAISED BEEF BARBACOA 104

CARNITAS 106

CARNE GUISADA 103

POLLO CON MOLE 107

MOLE POBLANO SAUCE 109

THE WIDE WORLD OF SALSA:

AVOCADO CREMA 111 | PICO DE GALLO 112 |
COWBOY GRINGO TABLE HOT SAUCE 112 | ROASTED TOMATO SALSA 113 |
SALSA MACHA 113 | SALSA VERDE 116 | SUPER-SPICY
"STAFF ONLY" SALSA 116 | TOMATILLO CRUDO 117

Standard
TEX-MEX TACOS

are really just the classic crispy beef taco: a U-shaped fried corn shell stuffed with a spicy ground beef filling and topped with shredded lettuce, cheese, and diced tomatoes. Once fajitas became popular in the 1980s, a lot of restaurants began offering fajita tacos—both beef and chicken, aka *tacos al carbón*. But Tex-Mex menus have broadly expanded in the past fifteen years. Though you still find your classic crispy beef tacos, now you can choose from a wider range of options, including flour or corn tortillas and fillings such as *carnitas*, grilled fish, carne asada, and barbacoa—all of which are traditional Mexican preparations.

There are three basic parts to a taco and I cover each in this chapter: the vessel, which could be a corn or flour tortilla or a crispy or puffy shell; the fillings, which could be just about anything (but we'll stick to the most common ones); and the toppings, including salsas, lettuce, cheese, and more (we'll primarily dive into salsas).

FLOUR
TORTILLAS
PAGE 101

CORN TORTILLAS PAGE 98

WITH ORIGINAL TEX-MEX CUISINE, the options for tacos were limited to the kind you find in a crispy shell. But as it evolved—and a sister cuisine called Cali-Mex developed—so did the taco offerings. In more recent years, as authentic Mexican food has made its mark on American culture, it's hard to know which tacos are Tex, which are Mex, and which are Cali. Here's a quick guide to some of the more common tacos seen today.

TEX-MEX

Though corn tortillas factor heavily in Tex-Mex food overall, flour tortillas are often the base for its tacos.

CRISPY TACO
PUFFY TACO
FAJITA TACO
AL CARBÓN
BREAKFAST TACO

TRADITIONAL MEXICAN

The simplest Mexican tacos rely on thin corn tortillas—sometimes two stacked together—to carry meat, and they're topped with just a sprinkle of cilantro and chopped white onion.

AL PASTOR

BARBACOA

CAMARONES (SHRIMP) DIABLO

CARNE ASADA

CARNITAS

CHICKEN *TINGA*

CHICKEN OR PORK MOLE

COCHINITA PIBIL

FISH TACO
BURRITO TACO

As much as I'd love to claim it, the fish taco is just not Tex-Mex. It's strictly a Baja California creation.

CALI-MEX

THERE'S NO WRONG WAY TO TACO

DIY TACOS →

The Truth is,

YOU CAN MAKE A TACO OUT OF JUST ABOUT ANY PROTEIN OR VEGETABLE IN THIS BOOK. But it's what you put atop that protein that makes the taco special. Here's a guide to building the perfect taco, from tortilla and filling to salsa and other toppings, every time. Feel free to experiment on your own, too.

CRISPY BEEF TACO

Crispy Taco Shell
(page 97)

Beef Picadillo (page 106)

Shredded lettuce

Diced tomato

Shredded cheese

Roasted Tomato Salsa
(page 113)

~~~~~

PUFFY TACO

Puffy Taco Shell (page 98)

Beef Picadillo (page 106)

Shredded lettuce

Diced tomato

Shredded cheese

Cowboy Gringo Table Hot Sauce
(page 112)

Chile con Queso (page 72)

~~~~~

BEEF FAJITA TACO

Flour Tortilla (page 101)

Beef Fajitas (page 181)

Sautéed onions and poblano
peppers

Sour cream

Lettuce

Pico de Gallo (page 112)

Tomatillo Crudo (page 117)

BREAKFAST TACO

Flour Tortilla (page 101)

Refried Beans (page 61)

Chihuahua or Monterrey
Jack cheese

Egg

San Antonio-Style Breakfast
Salsa (page 36)

~~~~~

AL PASTOR

Corn Tortilla (page 98)

Al Pastor (page 196)

Chopped grilled pineapple

Avocado Crema (page 111)

~~~~~

BARBACOA

Corn Tortilla (page 98)

Braised Beef Barbacoa
(page 104)

Tomatillo Crudo (page 117)

Lime

~~~~~

CARNE ASADA

Corn Tortilla (page 98)

Carne Asada (page 186)

Guacamole (page 68)

Chopped onion

Roasted Tomato Salsa
(page 113)

CARNE GUISADA

Corn Tortilla (page 98)

Carne Guisada (page 103)

Sliced avocado

Salsa Verde (page 118)

~~~~~

CARNITAS

Corn Tortilla (page 98)

Carnitas (page 106)

Cilantro

Chopped onion

Salsa Verde (page 116)

~~~~~

CHICKEN OR PORK MOLE

Corn Tortilla (page 98)

Chicken or Pork Mole (page 107
and 109)

Sliced onion

Toasted sesame

~~~~~

FISH TACO

Corn Tortilla (page 98)

Whole Grilled Red Snapper
(page 168)

Shredded cabbage

Tomatillo Crudo (page 117)

SPICY MAYO: 2 parts
mayonnaise, 1 part Super-Spicy
"Staff Only" Salsa (page 116)

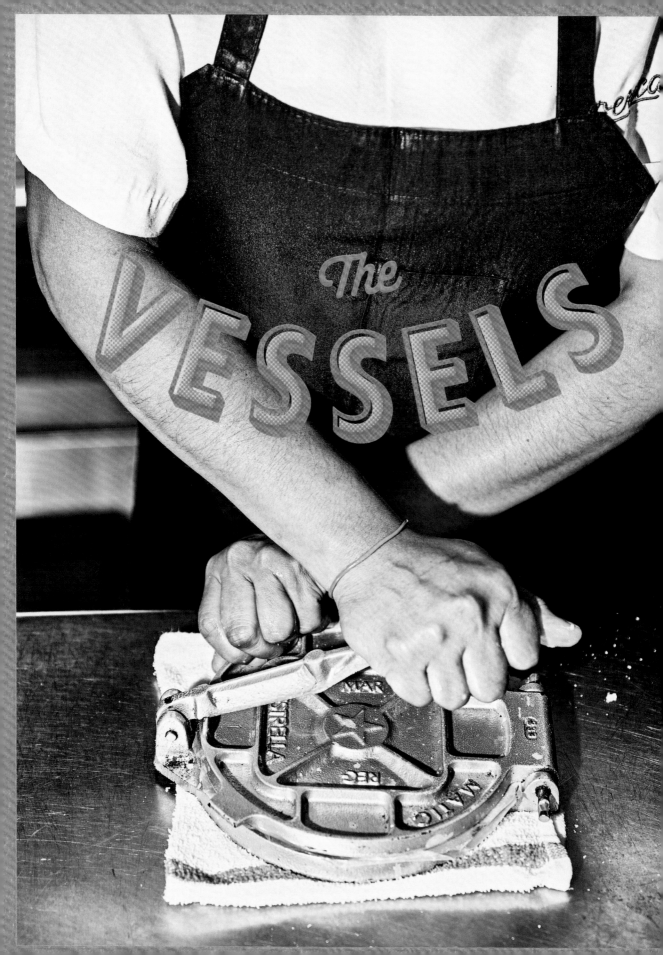

TORTILLAS
SOFT AND CRISPY

ANY GOOD TEX-MEX RESTAURANT worth its salt makes its own tortillas—both corn and flour—in-house. The corn variety should be pliant and rich with corn flavor, while flour tortillas should be light and fluffy, as well as thin, soft, and a little translucent. Freshly made flour tortillas are sublime. A good rule to follow when eating out: Ask if the flour tortillas are made in-house. If not, go with the corn!

Beyond these soft tortillas, there are also the crispy and the puffy, two hallmarks of Tex-Mex cuisine. With the crispy taco shell, take advantage of the firm U-shaped structure; it allows you to more easily hold the taco in one hand. Once it's in your hand, you shouldn't have to put it down. You should be able to finish it in four bites at most—well, maybe just two, but who's counting?

The puffy taco is most commonly associated with San Antonio; you won't find this style as much throughout the rest of Texas. What's cool about a puffy taco is that the masa is slid into hot oil rather than griddled, which causes it to become very airy. The outside is delicate and crunchy, while the inside is slightly chewy. The corn flavor is highlighted a lot more than in a griddled crispy taco.

CRISPY TACO SHELLS
Makes 12 shells

Vegetable oil
12 (6-inch) corn tortillas, store-bought or homemade (page 98)
Kosher salt

1 Fill a large Dutch oven or other heavy pot with oil to a depth of 1½ inches. Heat the oil over medium-high heat to 375°F. Line a wire rack with paper towels, place it on a baking sheet, and set it nearby.

2 Place a tortilla in the hot oil. Fry until golden, 10 to 15 seconds, then, using heat-resistant tongs, gently grab one side of the tortilla and fold it in half to create a U-shape. Hold it in place in the oil until the tortilla maintains its shape, 1 to 2 minutes. Fry until the tortilla is golden and crispy, 2 to 3 minutes more. Using the tongs, transfer it to the prepared rack and sprinkle it with salt. Repeat to fry the remaining tortillas.

3 Serve immediately.

TIP Masa harina can be found at most grocery stores and online.

CORN TORTILLAS

Makes 12 6-inch tortillas

2 cups masa harina (see Tip, page 97), plus more as needed
1½ teaspoons kosher salt

1 In a medium bowl, combine the masa harina, salt, and 2 cups water and stir until a dough forms. Turn out the dough onto a clean counter or cutting board. Using your hands, stir and knead the dough until it has the texture of Play-Doh, 3 to 4 minutes. To test the texture, roll a small ball of dough between the palms of your hands, then press it between your fingers. If the edges crack, it's too dry; if it sticks to your skin, it's too wet. Work in more water or masa harina as needed.

2 Divide the dough into 12 equal portions and use your hands to roll them into golf-ball-size rounds. Carefully flatten each round by hand to about ⅛-inch thickness. Stack them on a plate and cover them with a clean kitchen towel to prevent them from drying out.

3 Heat a well-seasoned griddle over medium-high heat.

4 Slice open the sides of a resealable plastic bag, creating a rectangle. Lay one end of the plastic rectangle on the bottom of a tortilla press. Place one piece of dough on the plastic, fold the other side of the plastic over the dough, and press to form a 6-inch tortilla. (Alternatively, use the bottom of a heavy cast-iron skillet to press the dough.) Carefully peel the tortilla from the plastic and place it on the heated griddle. Cook until the bottom is golden, about 30 seconds, then flip and cook the other side until dried, about 30 seconds more. The tortilla may puff up and brown lightly in spots. Stack the tortillas as they are cooked and wrap them in a clean kitchen towel or put them in a tortilla holder to trap the heat and steam.

5 Serve immediately.

PUFFY TACO SHELLS

Makes 12 shells / Serves 4

Vegetable oil
12 (6-inch) corn tortillas, store-bought or homemade
Kosher salt

1 Fill a large Dutch oven or other heavy pot with oil to a depth of 1½ inches. Heat the oil over medium-high heat to 375°F. Line a wire rack with paper towels, place it on a baking sheet, and set it nearby.

2 Slide a tortilla into the hot oil and, using a large metal spoon, carefully spoon the hot oil over the top of the shell, continuously basting the tortilla until it begins to puff, 10 to 15 seconds. Use the spoon to gently push down the middle of the puffed top to create a crease for fillings. Once the crease is set, fry the tortilla, continuously basting it with the hot oil, until golden and crispy, about 1 minute more. Using a slotted spoon, carefully transfer the shell to the prepared rack and sprinkle it with salt. Repeat to fry the remaining tortillas.

3 Serve immediately.

TIP

If you're not able to make your own corn tortillas, try to find fresh ones from a local Tex-Mex restaurant, or you can buy them at the store as a last resort. Just know they will likely not puff up as much.

FLOUR TORTILLAS

Makes 10 to 12 6-inch tortillas

2 ⅓ cups all-purpose flour, plus more for dusting

1 tablespoon baking powder

2 ¼ teaspoons kosher salt

⅔ cup vegetable shortening or lard

⅔ cup warm water

1 In the bowl of a stand mixer fitted with the paddle attachment, combine the flour, baking powder, and salt. Mix on low speed until well combined, 30 seconds. Add the shortening and mix on low speed until the mixture looks like coarse cornmeal, about 1 minute more. Add the water and mix on low speed until the dough comes together.

2 Switch to the dough hook attachment and mix on medium-high speed until the dough pulls away from the side of the bowl and springs back when you try to pull a piece off (you want the dough to fight you a little), 5 to 7 minutes. Cover the bowl with a damp kitchen towel and let the dough rest at room temperature for 30 minutes.

3 Divide the dough into 10 equal portions and use your hands to roll them into rounds slightly smaller than golf balls. Put them on a baking sheet, cover with a clean kitchen towel, and let rest for 30 minutes.

4 Place the dough balls in a medium bowl, sprinkle them lightly with flour, and toss to coat.

5 Heat a well-seasoned griddle over medium-high heat. When the griddle is hot, transfer a dough ball to a lightly floured surface and use a rolling pin to roll it out as thin as possible. Add one tortilla and cook until it is puffed and golden brown spots appear on the bottom, about 1 minute. Flip and cook until brown spots begin to form, 30 seconds more. If bubbles form in the dough, pop the bubbles with a paring knife to deflate them. Repeat with the remaining dough balls. Stack the tortillas as they are cooked and wrap them in a clean kitchen towel or put them in a tortilla holder to trap the heat and steam.

6 Serve warm.

TIP

If using store-bought flour tortillas, I like to heat them on a griddle as I do fresh ones. It gives them a little more color and charred flavor. But if you're crunched for time, place **10 to 12 tortillas** in an insulated fabric tortilla warmer—or two clean dish towels—and microwave until warm, about **30 seconds**.

THE VESSELS

CARNE GUISADA

Makes enough to fill 4 to 6 tacos

Good *carne guisada* (beef stew) is one of the best cures for the common cold in the dead of winter. I like when it's cooked more like a roux-thickened stew rather than meat simmered in a thin broth. It's not exactly a pretty dish, but that's never stopped me from digging into a plate of it. Serve it with a side of fluffy flour tortillas, either to wrap the stew into a taco or simply to sop up the gravy on the plate.

1½ pounds beef chuck, cut into 1-inch-thick slices

1 tablespoon kosher salt, plus more to taste

1 pound vine-ripened tomatoes, halved

1 pound tomatillos, husks removed, halved

3 jalapeño peppers, stemmed

1 poblano pepper, stemmed

1 medium onion, halved

2 garlic cloves

1½ tablespoons vegetable oil, plus more for brushing

6 tablespoons Standard Chile Paste (page 66)

½ teaspoon ground cumin

½ teaspoon freshly ground black pepper

½ teaspoon dried Mexican oregano

1½ tablespoons all-purpose flour

1 Preheat the oven to 375°F. Heat a grill to high or heat a grill pan over high heat.

2 Place the meat in a medium bowl, season with the salt, and toss to combine. Cover with a clean kitchen towel and set aside at room temperature while preparing the vegetables.

3 Brush the tomatoes, tomatillos, jalapeños, poblano, onion, and garlic lightly with oil. Grill until lightly charred, 8 to 10 minutes. Transfer the vegetables to a food processor and add the chile paste, cumin, black pepper, oregano, and ½ cup water. Process until smooth, 2 to 3 minutes.

4 Heat the oil in a 5-quart Dutch oven set over medium-high heat. When the oil shimmers, add the flour and cook, whisking continuously, until the mixture turns the color of milk chocolate, 4 to 5 minutes. Add the vegetable mixture, increase the heat to high, and bring to a boil. Add the meat, cover, and transfer the pot to the oven.

5 Roast until the meat is tender, 1½ to 2 hours. Taste and add more salt as needed.

6 If not using immediately, store the carne guisada in an airtight container in the refrigerator for 1 to 2 days. Before serving, reheat in a saucepan over medium heat until warmed through.

BRAISED BEEF BARBACOA

Makes enough to fill 8 tacos

Traditionally, *barbacoa* comes from the Caribbean and coastal parts of Central America, including Mexico. Whole lamb or sheep are commonly used on the islands, but as the method of cooking moved its way up through Northern Mexico and into Texas, beef head became more common. Today, you see *barbacoa* fairly regularly on menus—it's even available at Chipotle—but the meat is more likely to be beef stew meat or roast rather than beef head.

1 pound boneless beef short rib (chuck or stew meat)
Kosher salt and freshly ground black pepper
2 tablespoons vegetable oil
4 cups chicken broth
2 tablespoons fresh lime juice
1 cup chopped vine-ripened tomatoes
½ large onion, chopped
4 smoked dried pasilla chiles, stemmed
2 jalapeño peppers, stemmed and cut crosswise into 1-inch slices
3 garlic cloves, smashed
1 cinnamon stick
1 tablespoon ground cumin
1 tablespoon chili powder (I like Gebhardt)
1 bay leaf

1 Preheat the oven to 325°F.

2 Season the meat generously with salt and black pepper.

3 Heat the oil in a 4- to 5-quart Dutch oven or other heavy pot set over medium-high heat. When the oil shimmers, add the meat and cook until browned on all sides, 3 to 4 minutes per side. Transfer the meat to a plate.

4 Add the broth, lime juice, tomatoes, onion, pasillas, jalapeños, garlic, cinnamon stick, cumin, chili powder, and bay leaf to the pot. Bring to a boil over high heat. Remove the pot from the heat and add the beef, submerging it in the liquid. Cover and transfer to the oven. Braise until the meat is fork-tender, 2½ to 3 hours.

5 Transfer the meat to a large bowl. Using two forks, shred the meat into small pieces. Strain the liquid left in the pot, discarding the solids. Taste the liquid and season it with salt and pepper as needed. Pour the strained liquid over the meat.

6 If not using immediately, store the barbacoa in an airtight container in the refrigerator for 1 to 2 days. Before serving, reheat the meat in a saucepan over medium heat until warmed through.

BEEF PICADILLO

Makes enough to fill 6 tacos

THE FILLINGS

This taco meat is really the core ingredient for a lot of Tex-Mex dishes—enchiladas, tostadas, flautas, tamales, and more. But the primary home for this spicy ground beef mixture is in the taco. I have some pretty strong opinions when it comes to crispy beef picadillo tacos, and the most important thing is that the meat be moist and flavorful. Don't make the mistake of letting it dry out as it simmers on the stove. When the beef is done, there should be a layer of liquid along the bottom of the pan.

2 tablespoons vegetable oil
1 onion, chopped
1 garlic clove, minced
1 jalapeño pepper, chopped
1 pound ground beef
2 vine-ripened tomatoes, chopped
1 tablespoon chili powder (I like Gebhardt)
1 tablespoon ground cumin
Kosher salt and freshly ground black pepper
1 cup dark beer (I like Modelo Negra), plus more as needed

1 Heat the oil in a large skillet set over medium heat. Add the onion, garlic, and jalapeño and cook, stirring frequently, until the onion is translucent, 4 to 5 minutes. Add the beef and cook, using a wooden spoon to break up the meat as it browns, for 6 to 8 minutes. Drain the mixture, return it to the skillet, and set the skillet over medium heat. Add the tomatoes, chili powder, and cumin, season with salt and pepper, and cook, stirring occasionally, until the mixture is fragrant and well incorporated, 4 to 5 minutes.

2 Pour in the beer, bring to a simmer, and cook until the sauce begins to thicken, 15 to 20 minutes. If the meat starts to look dry, pour in a little more beer, ¼ cup at a time. You want the cooked beef to be wet.

3 If not using immediately, store the beef in an airtight container in the refrigerator for 1 to 2 days. Before serving, reheat the meat in a saucepan over medium heat until warmed through.

CARNITAS

Makes enough to fill 8 tacos

Spanish for "little meats," *carnitas* is a great way to deliciously feed a lot of people with a humble piece of pork. The first step in the cooking process keeps things slow and low, with the meat submerged in lard and cooked until it becomes super rich and tender. But what elevates *carnitas* is then taking that meat and crisping it up by frying it in a skillet before you serve it. It develops a great crunchy texture that makes the flavor come alive.

1 tablespoon kosher salt
1 tablespoon sugar
1 teaspoon garlic powder
1 teaspoon ground cumin
¼ teaspoon freshly ground black pepper
3 pounds pork belly, skin removed
¾ cup lard (page 26), melted

1 Preheat the oven to 300°F.

2 In a small bowl, combine the salt, sugar, garlic powder, cumin, and pepper. Rub the seasoning mixture all over the pork belly. Place the pork in a small roasting pan, spoon in the lard all around, cover tightly with aluminum foil, and roast until the meat is fork-tender, about 2 hours. Remove the pan from the oven and let cool slightly. Cover the pan and refrigerate until completely chilled, at least 4 hours or up to overnight.

3 If not using immediately, store the pork and lard in an airtight container in the refrigerator for 1 to 2 days.

4 When ready to use, remove the pork from the lard and set aside. Transfer the lard to a large heavy pot set over high heat and bring it to 365°F. Cut the pork into 1-inch cubes and carefully place them in the hot lard. Fry until crispy and golden brown, 4 to 5 minutes. Using a slotted spoon, transfer the pork to a cutting board and coarsely chop. Serve hot.

POLLO CON MOLE

Makes enough to fill 8 tacos

Mole is a traditional Mexican sauce that can take many forms and showcase many different chiles, seeds, fruits, and nuts. The most common version served in America is mole poblano, but I never saw it much in Tex-Mex restaurants in the 1980s and '90s. The first time I encountered it, I wasn't really a fan. It was too brown and, honestly, a little scary—it looked like chocolate smeared on chicken. Later I learned to appreciate the complexity of it—traditional recipes often contain more than two dozen ingredients. It's not hard to make, but you need patience.

8 bone-in, skin-on chicken thighs
Kosher salt and freshly ground black pepper
2 tablespoons vegetable oil
2 cups mole poblano sauce, store-bought or homemade (page 109)

1 Preheat the oven to 400°F.

2 Season the chicken on both sides with salt and pepper.

3 Heat the oil in a large cast-iron skillet over medium-high heat. When the oil shimmers, add the chicken, skin-side down, and cook until golden brown, 5 to 6 minutes. Flip the chicken and cook until browned on the second side, about 1 minute. Transfer the chicken to a plate.

4 Carefully discard the oil from the skillet. Pour in 1 cup water and use a wooden spoon to scrape up the browned bits from the bottom of the skillet. Set the skillet over medium-high heat, add the mole, bring to a simmer, and cook for about 2 minutes until heated through.

5 Return the chicken to the skillet, skin-side up. Place the skillet in the oven and roast until the chicken is just cooked through, 25 to 30 minutes. Cover with aluminum foil toward the end of the baking time if the mole begins to get too dark.

6 Transfer the chicken to a cutting board and let cool slightly. Using 2 forks, pull the meat from the bone and coarsely chop (discard the bones), then return it to the skillet with the mole.

7 If not using immediately, store the chicken and mole in an airtight container in the refrigerator for 1 to 2 days. Before serving, reheat in a saucepan over medium heat until warmed through.

POLLO
CON MOLE
PAGE 107

MOLE POBLANO SAUCE

Makes about 3½ cups

6 ounces dried ancho chiles (about 12), stemmed, some seeds removed

3 ounces dried guajillo chiles (about 20), stemmed, some seeds removed

½ ounce dried morita chiles (about 4), stemmed, some seeds removed

Boiling water

1 corn tortilla (6-inch), store-bought or homemade (page 98)

2 tablespoons unsalted butter

1 tablespoon chopped walnuts

1 tablespoon chopped pecans

1 tablespoon sesame seeds

¾ teaspoon coriander seeds

¾ teaspoon aniseeds

¾ teaspoon whole black peppercorns

1 cinnamon stick

¼ teaspoon whole cloves

¼ teaspoon allspice berries

2 tablespoons raisins

1 ripe small plantain

½ cup roasted tomato salsa, store-bought or homemade (page 113)

1 tablespoon packed light brown sugar

1 (3-ounce) disc Mexican chocolate, coarsely chopped

1 teaspoon kosher salt, plus more to taste

Place the ancho, guajillo, and morita chiles in a small bowl and cover with boiling water. Cover the bowl and soak for 30 minutes.

Meanwhile, heat a grill to high.

Grill the tortilla until charred on both sides, 1 to 2 minutes. Set aside.

In a large sauté pan set over medium heat, melt the butter. Add the walnuts, pecans, sesame seeds, coriander, aniseeds, peppercorns, cinnamon stick, cloves, and allspice. Cook, stirring continuously, until the nuts and seeds are golden in color and the spices are fragrant, 4 to 5 minutes. Remove and discard the cinnamon stick. Transfer the mixture to a mini food processor or blender and process until finely chopped, 1 to 2 minutes. Add the raisins and the plantain and process until smooth, about 2 minutes. Set aside.

Drain the chiles in a strainer set over a bowl; reserve the soaking liquid. Transfer the chiles to a blender and add ¼ cup of the reserved liquid. Purée until smooth, adding more liquid as needed, ¼ cup at a time, so the sauce has a thin, pastelike consistency but is not runny. Pass the purée through a fine-mesh strainer into a large saucepan.

Add the grilled tortilla and the spiced nut-seed mixture to the saucepan. Stir in the salsa, brown sugar, chocolate, salt, and 1 cup water. Set the pan over low heat and slowly bring the mixture to a simmer, about 30 minutes. Simmer until the chocolate has melted and the tortilla is very soft, about 30 minutes more. Using an immersion blender, purée until smooth. If the mole is too thick, add more water, ¼ cup at a time, until thinned to the desired consistency. Taste and add more salt as needed.

If not using immediately, store the mole in an airtight container in the refrigerator for up to about a week. Before serving, reheat in a saucepan over medium heat until warmed through.

the
TOPPINGS

THE WIDE WORLD OF
SALSA

IF YOU ASK ME, salsa—that smooth and spicy marriage of tomato, onion, and pepper—is the central element in Tex-Mex cooking. Whether it's served as a dip for tortilla chips or a condiment for tacos or used as a sauce for broiling enchiladas, salsa, in all its forms, is the spark that brings Tex-Mex cuisine alive.

Coinciding with the rise of Tex-Mex in the 1980s, salsa itself became so popular that, by 1992, it had dethroned ketchup as the top-selling condiment in America, according to a report from the market research firm Packaged Facts. As ubiquitous as it has become, salsa is generally thought just to be a red-hued, somewhat liquid mixture made primarily of tomatoes. That, my friends, is far from the whole story. *Salsa* means "sauce," and it can vary widely in color—from the recognizable red to green, orange, smoky red-brown, and even brown—thanks to ingredients such as tomatillos, avocado, herbs, and the wide variety of chiles that may be added to the mix. And this is where it really gets exciting, since the resulting flavors are bold and unique.

What follows is a selection of staple salsas I like to have on hand to take anything from basic breakfast eggs to an at-home taco party to the next level.

AVOCADO CREMA
Makes about 1 cup

2 avocados, pitted and peeled
1 small jalapeño pepper, stemmed and coarsely chopped
1 garlic clove
1 tablespoon chopped fresh cilantro
½ teaspoon kosher salt, plus more to taste
Juice of 1 lime

1 In a blender or food processor, combine the avocados, jalapeño, garlic, cilantro, salt, lime juice, and 2 tablespoons water. Purée until smooth, stopping to scrape down the sides of the blender once or twice, 2 to 3 minutes. Taste and add more salt as needed.

2 Serve or store in an airtight container in the refrigerator for 2 to 3 days.

PICO DE GALLO

Makes about 2 cups

1¼ cups finely chopped onions
¼ cup finely chopped tomato
¼ cup minced jalapeño pepper
¼ cup chopped fresh cilantro
¼ cup fresh lime juice
½ teaspoon kosher salt, plus more to taste

1 In a large bowl, stir together the onion, tomato, jalapeño, cilantro, lime juice, and salt in a large bowl. Taste and add more salt as needed.

2 Serve or store in an airtight container in the refrigerator for up to 2 days.

COWBOY GRINGO TABLE HOT SAUCE

Makes about 2½ cups

2 cups white vinegar
1 ounce dried chiles de árbol (about 40), stemmed
1 ounce dried morita chiles (about 8), stemmed
3 garlic cloves
1 teaspoon whole black peppercorns
1 teaspoon dried Mexican oregano
2 whole cloves
Pinch of ground cumin

1 In a small saucepan set over high heat, combine the vinegar, chiles, garlic, peppercorns, oregano, cloves, cumin, and ½ cup water. Bring to a simmer, stirring occasionally. Reduce the heat to low and simmer, stirring occasionally, until the chiles have softened, about 5 minutes. Remove the pan from the heat and let cool for 30 minutes.

2 Transfer the mixture to a blender and purée until smooth, 2 minutes. Pour through a fine-mesh strainer (discard the solids).

3 Serve or store in an airtight container in the refrigerator for up to 1 month.

ROASTED TOMATO SALSA

Makes about 2 cups

1 pound vine-ripened tomatoes
¼ onion
3 small serrano peppers
1 garlic clove
2 tablespoons fresh cilantro leaves
1 teaspoon kosher salt, plus more to taste

1 Heat a grill to high, or place an oven rack 6 to 8 inches from the heat source and preheat the oven to broil. If using the broiler, line a baking sheet with aluminum foil.

2 Grill the tomatoes, onion, and serranos until charred all over, or place them on a baking sheet and broil, turning once, until charred, 8 to 10 minutes. Transfer the grilled vegetables to a blender and add the garlic, cilantro, and salt. Purée until almost smooth, about 1 minute.

3 Serve or store in an airtight container in the refrigerator for 2 to 3 days.

SALSA MACHA

Makes about 1½ cups

1 cup peanut oil
½ cup unsalted peanuts or almonds
4 garlic cloves, smashed
2 tablespoons sesame seeds
1.5 ounces dried guajillo chiles (about 10), stemmed, seeded, and torn into small pieces
.5 ounce dried chiles de árbol (about 20), stemmed, seeded, and torn into small pieces
1 tablespoon cider vinegar
1 tablespoon light brown sugar
⅛ teaspoon dried Mexican oregano
2 teaspoons kosher salt, plus more to taste
¼ cup grapeseed oil

1 In a 2-quart saucepan set over medium heat, combine the peanut oil, peanuts, garlic, and sesame seeds. Cook, stirring occasionally, until the garlic turns light golden, about 5 minutes. Remove the pot from the heat and stir in the dried chiles. Set aside to cool slightly, stirring occasionally.

2 Transfer the peanut mixture to a blender. Add the vinegar, brown sugar, oregano, and salt. Purée until a slightly loose paste forms, about 5 minutes. You should be able to see small dark flakes of chile in the mixture.

3 Pour the mixture into a small bowl and stir in the grapeseed oil until well combined. Taste and add more salt as needed.

4 Serve or store in an airtight container in the refrigerator for up to 3 weeks.

THE TOPPINGS

"VERDE"

"PICO DE GA

"ROASTED TOM

"AVO CREMA"

"COWBOY GRINGO"

"MAC

SALSA VERDE

Makes about 3 cups

1 pound tomatillos, husks removed

2 serrano peppers

1 small bunch cilantro, tough stems removed

1 garlic clove

1 teaspoon kosher salt, plus more to taste

2 tablespoons finely chopped onion

1 Heat a grill to high or heat a grill pan over high heat.

2 Grill the tomatillos until they're charred in several places but before they begin to turn grayish green, about 5 minutes. Transfer to a blender.

3 Grill the serranos until they're charred on all sides, about 3 minutes. Remove the stems and seeds and add the flesh to the blender.

4 Add the cilantro, garlic and salt to the blender and purée until smooth, about 1 minute. Transfer the salsa to a 1-quart container and fold in the onion. Taste and add more salt as needed.

5 Serve or store in an airtight container in the refrigerator for 2 to 3 days.

SUPER-SPICY "STAFF ONLY" SALSA

Makes about 1½ cups

1 large vine-ripened tomato

¼ cup vegetable oil

½ cup stemmed dried chiles de árbol

1 garlic clove

½ teaspoon chicken bouillon

¼ teaspoon ground cumin

½ teaspoon kosher salt, plus more to taste

1 Heat a grill to high, or place an oven rack 6 to 8 inches from the heat source and preheat the oven to broil. If using the broiler, line a baking sheet with aluminum foil.

2 Grill the tomato until charred on all sides, or place it on the prepared baking sheet and broil, turning once, until charred, 8 to 10 minutes. Set aside.

3 Heat the oil in a small heavy pot set over medium-high heat. When the oil shimmers, add the chiles and cook, stirring, until they turn slightly darker in color, 15 to 20 seconds.

4 Carefully discard most of the oil from the pot and carefully add enough water just to cover the chiles. Set the pot over high heat, bring the water to a boil, and cook until the chiles have softened, 5 to 7 minutes. Drain the water.

5 In a blender, combine the tomato, chiles, garlic, bouillon, cumin, and salt. Purée until smooth, about 1 minute. Taste and add more salt as needed.

6 Serve or store in an airtight container in the refrigerator for up to 1 week.

TOMATILLO CRUDO

Makes about 5 cups

1½ pounds tomatillos, husks removed, cut in half

1 avocado, pitted and peeled

2 or 3 serrano peppers, stemmed

¼ small onion, coarsely chopped

2 garlic cloves

1 large bunch cilantro, tough stems removed

1½ teaspoons kosher salt, plus more to taste

1 In a blender, combine the tomatillos, avocado, serranos, onion, garlic, cilantro, and salt. Purée until smooth, about 1 minute. Taste and add more salt as needed.

2 Serve or store in an airtight container in the refrigerator for 2 to 3 days.

OTHER THAN SALSAS,

there are a few other toppings that are standard in taco-building. If you're hosting a handful of friends, you'll also need:

2 cups shredded
ICEBERG LETTUCE

2 cups shredded
MILD CHEDDAR CHEESE

1½ cups chopped
TOMATO

½ cup chopped
WHITE ONION

¼ cup roughly chopped
FRESH CILANTRO

ENCHILADAS Y
TAMALES
Y MÁS

ENCHILADAS AND
TAMALES AND MORE

CHEESE ENCHILADAS CON
CHILI GRAVY 124

CHICKEN ENCHILADAS
CON MOLE 126

BEEF
ENCHILADA
129

ENCHILADAS SUIZAS 130

OLD SCHOOL
TAMALES
132

SPICY PORK
TAMALES
134

TOSTADAS 139

THE OG
NACHO
140

BARBACOA
FLAUTAS
143

CHILES
RELLENOS
144

ALBONDIGAS 148

WHEN I THINK OF Enchiladas,

I think of Tex-Mex restaurant scenes from my youth: trays of smoking-hot plates bearing pairs of stuffed tortillas, smothered in enchilada gravy and with a layer of melted cheddar cheese bubbling on top, whizzing around the dining room on their way to hungry diners. In Tex-Mex cuisine, enchiladas hold a revered status, and they share their fame with tamales, tostadas, nachos, and of course, tacos. It doesn't matter which restaurant, cantina, or dive you stop into, you'll find all these on the menu, either à la carte or as part of a combo plate (page 123).

CHEESE ENCHILADAS
CON CHILI GRAVY
PAGE 124

COMBO PLATE

In Texas, most people have a regular neighborhood Tex-Mex haunt that serves up the standard queso, fajitas, and enchiladas, but no menu is complete without a list of combination platters, or combo plates. Some restaurants simply designate them #1, #2, or #3, while others name them after friends or family, like Lito's Plate and the Maggie Plate.

Each includes varying combinations of classic items such as tostadas, crispy beef tacos, enchiladas, and *tacos al carbón*, and they *always* include rice and beans. Though the crispy beef taco or tostada often comes on the side to preserve the chilled lettuce and tomato, the rest of the items arrive on a big oval plate, with a final sprinkle of shredded cheese on top, dissolving into a glistening pool of grease that makes everything appear as if it's melted together.

The average combo plate typically includes more food than any one person should really eat, but it really does offer a way to taste a tailored selection of classic Tex-Mex items in one sitting.

CHEESE ENCHI...

Vegetable oil, for softening tortillas

10 (6-inch) corn tortillas, store-bought or homemade (page 98)

2 cups Chili Gravy (recipe opposite)

1 cup grated American cheese

1½ cups grated cheddar cheese

2 tablespoons chopped onion

1 tablespoon unsalted butter

4 large eggs

CHILI GRAVY is a true Tex-Mex creation. Developed in the early days of the cuisine, it falls somewhere between a chili con carne and a roux-based gravy. Some say its smoky chiles, cumin, and garlic characteristics feel Mexican, but its mild flavor and tempered spiciness make it more approachable to the American palate. Sometimes seen in stores labeled as "enchilada sauce," this condiment is used on a number of Tex-Mex dishes, from tamales to tacos, though its signature pairing is over a cheese enchilada.

1 Preheat the oven to 400°F.

2 Fill a Dutch oven or large heavy pot with oil to a depth of ½ inch. Heat the oil over medium-high heat to 365°F. Using tongs, dip a few tortillas at a time into the hot oil until softened, 3 or 4 seconds. Stack them on a plate and cover them with a clean kitchen towel to keep warm.

3 Spread ⅓ cup of the gravy over the bottom of an 8 x 12-inch baking dish.

4 In a medium bowl, combine the American cheese and 1 cup of the cheddar. Place a softened tortilla on a clean work surface, spoon ¼ cup of the cheese blend down the center, and roll it up to enclose the cheese. Place the rolled tortilla seam-side down in the prepared dish. Repeat with the remaining tortillas and cheese blend. Top the enchiladas with the remaining gravy. Sprinkle evenly with the remaining ½ cup cheddar.

5 Bake until the cheese on top has melted and the casserole is bubbling around the edges, 15 to 20 minutes. Remove the enchiladas from the oven and top with the onion. Let cool slightly.

6 Meanwhile, melt the butter in a medium sauté pan set over medium heat. Once the butter has melted, crack the eggs directly into the pan. Reduce the heat to low, cover, and cook until the whites are completely set but the yolks are still runny, 4 to 5 minutes.

7 Top the enchiladas with the eggs and serve immediately.

LADAS *con* CHILI GRAVY

CHILI GRAVY

MAKES ABOUT 6 CUPS

1 large onion, coarsely chopped

10 garlic cloves

1 pound ground beef

½ cup vegetable oil

½ cup all-purpose flour

½ cup Standard Chile Paste (page 66)

1½ teaspoons beef bouillon

5 tablespoons chili powder (I like Gebhardt)

1 tablespoon ground cumin

1 teaspoon dried Mexican oregano

½ teaspoon ground cloves

1½ tablespoons kosher salt

1 tablespoon freshly ground black pepper

In a blender or food processor, combine the onion, garlic, and 3 cups water. Purée until smooth, about 30 seconds. Transfer the mixture to a large saucepan over medium-high heat. Add the ground beef and bring to a simmer, using a wooden spoon to break up the meat as it cooks. Reduce the heat to medium-low and simmer until the beef is cooked through and the mixture is almost dry, 45 to 50 minutes.

Meanwhile, in a small sauté pan set over medium heat, whisk together the oil and flour. Cook, whisking continuously, until the roux is blond in color, 5 minutes. Remove the pan from the heat.

Add the roux, chile paste, bouillon, chili powder, cumin, oregano, cloves, salt, pepper, and 3 cups water to the meat mixture and stir to combine. Bring to a simmer over medium heat and cook until the flavors meld and the mixture has the consistency of a thin gravy, 5 to 10 minutes.

Use immediately, or let cool completely and store in an airtight container in the refrigerator for 2 to 3 days.

CHICKEN Enchiladas CON MOLE

This is simply another way to enjoy the richness of mole. In Oaxaca, Mexico, these are called *enmoladas* for the addition of mole as the featured sauce. Traditionally, the tortillas are dipped in the mole first before they are rolled with fillings and broiled. The mole is then drizzled over the enchiladas when they are served. Personally, I like to let the mole bake into cheesy gooeyness instead.

Cooking spray

Vegetable oil, for softening tortillas

8 (6-inch) corn tortillas, store-bought or homemade (page 98)

2 cups mole poblano sauce, store-bought or homemade (page 109)

1 cup Shredded Smoked Chicken (recipe follows) or shredded store-bought rotisserie chicken

½ cup shredded Chihuahua cheese

½ cup crumbled queso fresco

¼ cup sesame seeds, toasted

1 Place a rack 6 to 8 inches from the heat source and preheat the oven to broil. Spray an 8 x 12-inch baking dish with cooking spray.

2 Fill a Dutch oven or large heavy pot with oil to a depth of ½ inch. Heat the oil over medium-high heat to 350°F.

3 Using tongs, dip a few tortillas at a time into the hot oil until softened, 3 or 4 seconds. Stack them on a plate and cover with a clean kitchen towel to keep warm.

4 In a small saucepan set over medium heat, heat the mole until heated through, 5 to 6 minutes. Remove the pan from the heat and cover to keep the mole hot.

5 If the chicken is cold, wrap it in aluminum foil and heat it in the oven until warmed through, 5 minutes.

6 Place a softened tortilla on a clean work surface, spoon 2 tablespoons of the chicken down the center, and roll it up to enclose the chicken. Place the rolled tortilla seam-side down in the prepared baking dish. Repeat with the remaining tortillas and chicken. Top the enchiladas with the mole and sprinkle with the Chihuahua cheese.

7 Broil until the cheese is golden and bubbling, about 5 minutes. Top with the queso fresco and sesame seeds and serve warm.

TIP To toast sesame seeds, place them in a small dry skillet over medium-high heat and cook, jostling the pan regularly to keep the seeds from burning, until they brown slightly, 2 to 3 minutes. Do not leave them unattended, as they can burn quickly. Transfer the seeds to a plate and set them aside until ready to use.

SHREDDED SMOKED CHICKEN

MAKES 2 CUPS

¼ cup kosher salt, plus more as needed

1 tablespoon sugar

2 bone-in, skin-on chicken breasts

Vegetable oil, for brushing

In a medium bowl, combine the salt and sugar. Add 1 quart water and stir until the salt and sugar have dissolved. Add the chicken breasts, cover, and refrigerate overnight or for at least 8 hours.

When ready to cook the chicken, heat a grill to high or heat a grill pan over high heat.

Remove the chicken from the brine and pat dry. Brush the chicken all over with vegetable oil. Grill the chicken over direct heat for 3 minutes per side, then move the chicken to indirect heat and grill, uncovered, until a thermometer inserted into the thickest part reads 160°F, 15 to 20 minutes more. (Cover with the grill lid if the chicken is thick and needs more time.) Remove the chicken from the grill and let it cool slightly, about 5 minutes. Using two forks or tongs, shred the chicken into bite-size pieces.

If not using immediately, store the chicken in an airtight container in the refrigerator for 3 to 4 days.

BEEF ENCHILADA

SERVES 4

THE CLASSIC CHEESE ENCHILADA (see page 124) is what most people associate with old-school Tex-Mex, but the beef enchilada has always had a seat at the table. Similar in form to a cheese enchilada—a corn tortilla filled with cheese, rolled up, and topped with a chili con carne sauce or gravy and melted cheese—the beef variety is filled with beef picadillo, the same as you find in crispy beef tacos. It's an enchilada for beef lovers, and it's only complete with a sprinkle of finely chopped white onion and a few slices of avocado on the side.

1 Place a rack 6 to 8 inches from the heat source and preheat the oven to broil.

2 Fill a Dutch oven or large heavy pot with oil to a depth of ½ inch. Heat the oil over medium-high heat to 350°F.

3 Using tongs, dip a few tortillas at a time into the hot oil until softened, 3 or 4 seconds. Stack them on a plate and cover with a clean kitchen towel to keep warm.

4 Place a softened tortilla on a clean work surface, spoon 2 tablespoons of the picadillo down the center, and roll it up to enclose the beef. Place the tortilla seam-side down in a baking dish large enough to hold all the rolled tortillas in a single layer. Repeat with the remaining tortillas and picadillo. Ladle the chili gravy evenly over the tortillas and top with the cheese and onion.

5 Broil until the cheese is golden and bubbling, about 5 minutes. Serve warm.

Vegetable oil, for softening tortillas

8 (6-inch) corn tortillas, store-bought or homemade (page 98)

1 recipe Beef Picadillo (page 106)

2 cups Chili Gravy (page 125), hot, or store-bought salsa

4 ounces Chihuahua cheese, grated

¼ cup finely chopped onion

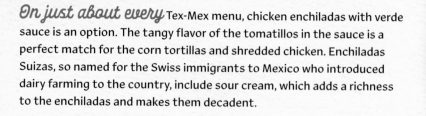

ENCHILADAS SUIZAS

On just about every Tex-Mex menu, chicken enchiladas with verde sauce is an option. The tangy flavor of the tomatillos in the sauce is a perfect match for the corn tortillas and shredded chicken. Enchiladas Suizas, so named for the Swiss immigrants to Mexico who introduced dairy farming to the country, include sour cream, which adds a richness to the enchiladas and makes them decadent.

SERVES 4

Cooking spray

1 (4-ounce) can crushed tomatillos

1 (4-ounce) can whole green chiles

¾ cup chopped poblano peppers

¾ cup chopped onion

¾ cup chopped fresh tomatillos

½ teaspoon finely chopped jalapeño pepper

2 teaspoons chopped fresh cilantro

1 garlic clove, minced

½ teaspoon kosher salt

Pinch of ground cloves

½ cup sour cream

Vegetable oil, for softening tortillas

8 (6-inch) corn tortillas, store-bought or homemade (page 98)

1 cup Shredded Smoked Chicken (page 128) or shredded store-bought rotisserie chicken

4 ounces Chihuahua cheese, grated

4 ounces queso fresco, crumbled

½ cup Cilantro Chimichurri (page 158) or additional chopped fresh cilantro

1 Place a rack 6 to 8 inches from the heat source and preheat the oven to broil. Spray an 8 x 12-inch baking dish with cook spray.

2 In a large saucepan set over medium-high heat, combine the canned tomatillos, green chiles, poblanos, onion, fresh tomatillos, jalapeño, cilantro, garlic, salt, and cloves. Bring to a boil, stirring occasionally. Reduce the heat to low and simmer until the vegetables have softened, 30 minutes. Using an immersion blender, purée the mixture until smooth. (Alternatively, carefully transfer the mixture to a regular blender and purée until smooth, then return it to the pan.) Stir in the sour cream to combine. Taste and add more salt as needed. Remove the pan from the heat and cover to keep the sauce warm.

3 Fill a Dutch oven or large heavy pot with oil to a depth of ½ inch. Heat the oil over medium-high heat to 350°F.

4 Using tongs, dip a few tortillas at a time into the hot oil until softened, 3 or 4 seconds. Stack them on a plate and cover with a clean kitchen towel to keep warm.

5 Place a softened tortilla on a clean work surface, spoon 2 tablespoons of the chicken down the center, and roll up to enclose the chicken. Place the rolled tortilla seam-side down in the prepared baking dish. Repeat with the remaining tortillas and chicken. Top the enchiladas with the sauce and sprinkle with the Chihuahua cheese.

6 Broil until the cheese is golden and bubbling, about 5 minutes.

7 Top with the queso fresco and chimichurri and serve warm.

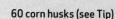

60 corn husks (see Tip)

2½ pounds boneless chuck roast, cut into 2-inch cubes

1 large onion, halved

5 garlic cloves, smashed

5 ancho chiles, stemmed

5 chiles de árbol, stemmed

1 teaspoon cumin seeds

2 tablespoons kosher salt, plus more to taste

1 tablespoon freshly ground black pepper

2 pounds masa, such as Maseca (see Tip)

9 ounces lard (see page 24)

Chili Gravy (page 125) or store-bought salsa

2 cups shredded mild cheddar cheese

THROUGH MUCH OF THE early twentieth century, tamales vendors were very common on the streets of South Texas towns and up through San Antonio. During the midmorning hours and through the afternoon, you'd hear them call, "Hot tamales!" along the street corners. They sold them out of a ten-gallon lard can for about a nickel apiece during the Depression. It was an easy way for an immigrant family to make an income.

When I was growing up, there was a guy in my neighborhood who drove around in a truck selling tamales just like your typical ice cream man. He was *our* tamales man. My mom would warm them up and smother them in her homemade chili gravy, or canned chili in a pinch. I don't have a tamale man these days, so I've developed a recipe based on the classics I grew up with that, for me, makes the ideal tamale.

1 Place the corn husks in a large baking dish and cover with warm water, making sure they are fully submerged, and soak overnight.

2 In a large pot or Dutch oven, combine the beef, onion, garlic, chiles, cumin, 1 tablespoon of the salt, and the pepper and cover with water by 1 inch. Set the pot over high heat and bring the water to a boil, stirring occasionally. Reduce the heat to low, cover, and simmer until the meat is fork-tender, about 90 minutes.

3 Transfer the meat to a plate and let cool slightly. Once it's cool enough to handle, use two forks to shred the beef into small pieces. Taste and add more salt as needed. Cover and set aside to cool completely.

4 Meanwhile, transfer the onion, garlic, and chiles from the cooking liquid to a blender (reserve the liquid) and purée until smooth.

School Tamales

TIPS

The ratio of masa to filling in a *tamal* is crucial. It's important to be generous with the filling, and you want to make sure the masa is fairly wet so the *tamal* doesn't dry out while it's cooking.

Corn husks and masa can be found at specialty Latin markets and online.

TIP

〰〰〰〰〰〰

Plan to soak the corn husks overnight before making the tamales. You may make the roast a day in advance. Just be sure to reheat in a saucepan over medium heat before assembling tamales.

5 Add 1½ cups of the vegetable purée to the shredded meat and stir to combine. Set aside.

6 In a large bowl, combine the masa, lard, and the remaining 1 tablespoon salt. Using your hands, mix and knead the masa until the lard is well incorporated and the mixture looks shaggy, 1 to 2 minutes. Gradually add enough of the reserved cooking liquid to create a dough similar in consistency to creamy mashed potatoes, 5 to 6 cups. Add ¼ cup of the vegetable purée to the masa and knead it into the dough until well incorporated. Cover the dough with a damp kitchen towel until you're ready to use it.

7 To assemble, remove a corn husk from the water and pat it dry. Set it smooth-side up on a clean work surface and spoon 2½ tablespoons of the masa into the center. Spread the masa into a thin layer. Spoon 1 tablespoon of the beef down the center of the masa, along the length of the husk. Fold one end of the husk over the filling, followed by the other side, enclosing the beef completely in the masa and the masa in the husk. Fold the bottom of the husk up. Lay the tamale on a baking sheet, cover with a damp kitchen towel, and repeat with the remaining ingredients.

8 Place a collapsible steamer basket in a large pot and add water just to reach the bottom of the basket. Carefully stand the tamales on their folded ends in the steamer basket, standing them next to one another so they do not fall over. Cover the pot and bring the water just to a boil over high heat. Reduce the heat to maintain a simmer and steam the tamales until the masa is firm and easily pulls away from the husk, about 90 minutes. Add water to the pot as needed to keep it from drying out.

9 Serve family-style with chili gravy and the cheddar alongside.

SPICY PORK TAMALES

MAKES ABOUT 48 TAMALES

There are a vast number of fillings you can use for tamales, three of the most common being poblano peppers, shredded pork, and Oaxaca cheese. While the tamales I grew up on included beef filling with chili gravy, it was more common to find red chile and shredded pork in places like El Paso in West Texas. It wasn't until a little later in life that I discovered them—we didn't spend a lot of time in West Texas when I was a kid. While I like the tamales of my childhood, I've found the slow burn of these spicy pork tamales to be just as enticing, if not a little more so.

60 corn husks (see Tip, page 133)

10 dried ancho chiles, stemmed

6 dried chiles de árbol, stemmed

2 dried morita or chipotle chiles, stemmed

Boiling water

2½ pounds boneless pork butt, cut into 2-inch chunks

1 large onion, quartered

8 garlic cloves, smashed

3 tablespoons kosher salt, plus more to taste

1 tablespoon freshly ground black pepper, plus more to taste

11 ounces lard (page 24)

¼ cup ground cumin

2 pounds masa, such as Maseca (see Tip, page 133)

Mole poblano sauce, store-bought or homemade (page 109)

2 cups shredded cheddar cheese

1 Place the corn husks in large baking dish and cover with warm water, making sure they are fully submerged, and soak overnight.

2 Place the ancho, árbol, and morita chiles in a bowl and cover with boiling water. Cover the bowl and set aside for 30 minutes.

3 Drain the chiles in a strainer set over a bowl; reserve the soaking liquid. Transfer the chiles and ½ cup of the reserved liquid to a blender and purée until smooth, about 1 minute. Add more of the soaking liquid if needed to create a paste consistency. Pass the chile paste through a fine-mesh strainer set over a bowl, using a spatula to press it through (discard the solids). Set aside.

4 Place the pork, onion, garlic, 2 tablespoons of the salt, and the pepper in a large pot and cover with water by one inch. Bring to a boil over high heat, stirring occasionally. Reduce the heat to low, cover, and simmer until the meat is fork-tender, about 90 minutes.

5 Transfer the meat to a plate and let cool slightly. Once it's cool enough to handle, use two forks to shred the pork into small pieces and set aside. Strain the cooking liquid (discard the solids) and set aside.

6 Melt 2 ounces of the lard in a large cast-iron skillet set over medium heat. When the lard shimmers, add the cumin and ½ cup of the chile paste and whisk to combine. Cook, whisking frequently, until fragrant, 3 to 4 minutes. Add the shredded pork and enough of the reserved cooking liquid to moisten the mixture, about ¾ cup. Taste and add more salt as needed. Cover and set aside to cool.

7 In a large bowl, combine the masa, the remaining 9 ounces lard, and remaining 1 tablespoon salt. Using your hands, mix and knead the masa until the lard is well incorporated and the mixture looks shaggy, 1 to 2 minutes. Gradually add enough of the reserved cooking liquid to create a dough similar in texture to creamy mashed potatoes, 5 to 6 cups. Add ¼ cup of the chile paste to the masa and knead it into dough until well incorporated. Cover the dough with a damp kitchen towel until you're ready to use it.

8 To assemble, remove a corn husk from the water and pat it dry. Set it smooth-side up on a clean work surface and spoon 2½ tablespoons of the masa into the center. Spread the masa into a thin layer. Spoon 1 tablespoon of the pork down the center of the masa. Fold one side of the husk over the filling, followed by the other side, enclosing the pork completely in the masa and the masa in the husk. Fold the bottom of the husk up. Lay the tamale on a baking sheet, cover with a damp kitchen towel, and repeat with the remaining ingredients.

9 Place a collapsible steamer basket in a large pot and add water just to reach the bottom of the basket. Carefully stand the tamales on their folded ends in the steamer basket, standing them next to one another so they do not fall over. Cover the pot and bring the water just to a boil over high heat. Reduce the heat to maintain a simmer and steam the tamales until the masa is firm and easily pulls away from the husk, about 90 minutes. Add water to the pot as needed to keep it from drying out.

10 Serve family-style with mole poblano sauce and the cheddar alongside.

TAMALES, TAMALADAS,
AND TAMALERAS

Over thousands of years leading up to Spanish colonization in the seventeenth century, Mesoamerican cultures (Aztec, Maya, Mixtec, and others) all made some form of banana-leaf- or corn-husk-wrapped packet of food similar to the modern-day tamale. Over time, tamales became associated with special occasions due to the time-intensive, community-involved process of making them.

Through the Spanish missions, this special-occasion dish was adopted into the Christian culture of Latin America, eventually becoming a keystone of one of the most important holidays on the Christian calendar, Christmas. The tradition has held strong through today, which is why you'll commonly find Mexican, Mexican Texan, and Mexican American families and friends gathering in kitchens big and small for annual *tamaladas*, or *tamal*-making parties, around the holidays.

At a *tamalada*, everyone from children to grandparents pitch in to help with the preparation, with each person assigned a task like making the filling, steaming the corn husks, preparing the masa, and so on. Then everyone comes together for a sort of choreographed assembly line, backed by festive music and filled with family banter and laughter (more laughter if tequila is involved), to stuff the tamales.

Such an assembly of *tamaleras*, tamale cooks, could easily churn out sixty dozen tamales in one day. The bounty is not only for the family to consume, but also to offer as gifts to friends throughout the holiday season. When I was growing up, homemade tamales from friends often made an appearance at holiday parties and almost always at the Christmas meal. Even if we were having the more traditional ham or turkey, tamales always had a place at the table.

TOSTADAS

TRADITIONALLY, if a Tex-Mex menu offers tostadas, it's referring to a corn tortilla that has been fried as a flat round rather than in a U-shape. You can usually expect a smear of refried beans on top and sometimes beef picadillo or shredded chicken topped with grated cheese. Some menus include the term *chalupas* instead of "tostadas." The truth is, a *chalupa* (Spanish for "canoe") is more of a Mexican item, particularly in the south-central part of the country, and it's made of fried ovals of masa that are shaped into a little canoe—hence the name—and served with a variety of toppings.

Vegetable oil, for frying

12 (6-inch) corn tortillas, store-bought or homemade (page 98)

Kosher salt

3 cups refried beans, store-bought or homemade (page 61)

4 cups Shredded Smoked Chicken (page 128) or shredded store-bought rotisserie chicken, or Beef Picadillo (page 106)

6 cups shredded lettuce

¾ cup chopped tomato

¾ cup crema Mexicana or sour cream

1 cup guacamole, store-bought or homemade (page 68)

¾ cup crumbled queso fresco

1 tablespoon dried Mexican oregano

24 sprigs fresh cilantro

1 Fill a 4-quart Dutch oven or other heavy pot with oil to a depth of 1 inch. Heat the oil over high heat to 375°F. Line a wire rack with paper towels, place it on a baking sheet, and set it nearby.

2 Gently slide a tortilla into the hot oil and fry it, basting the top or flipping it regularly, until it has stopped bubbling and become crisp, 2 to 3 minutes. Transfer the tortillas to the prepared rack and immediately sprinkle with salt. Repeat to fry the remaining tortillas.

3 Spread ¼ cup of the beans over each tostada, then top with equal parts chicken or picadillo, lettuce, tomato, crema, guacamole, and queso fresco. Garnish each tostada with a pinch of oregano and 2 sprigs of cilantro. Serve immediately.

THE ORIGINAL NACHO was the serendipitous creation of Ignacio Anaya, a restaurant owner in the small Mexican border town of Piedras Negras in 1943. As an off-menu appetizer for guests one evening, Anaya quartered a few tortillas, added a slice of cheddar cheese and a pickled jalapeño pepper to each, and broiled them in the oven. When asked the name of the tasty snack, he used his nickname and titled them "Nachos Especiales." These days, nachos come in every shape and size, from the "nacho mountain" (tortilla chips covered with melted cheese and piled high with an assortment of other toppings) to the "ballpark nacho" (tortilla chips doused in gloppy, bright orange stadium cheese). Personally, I prefer the old-school approach—and, of course, using good ingredients.

SERVES 4

Vegetable oil, for frying

8 (6-inch) corn tortillas, store-bought or homemade (page 98; see Note)

Kosher salt

1 cup refried beans, store-bought or homemade (page 61), warmed

1 cup grated Chihuahua, Monterey Jack, or cheddar cheese

16 to 32 pickled jalapeños, store-bought or homemade (page 62)

TIP

You can use store-bought tortilla chips instead of making your own: Spread 16 to 20 tortilla chips in a single layer over a foil-lined baking sheet and follow the remaining instructions as directed.

1 Place a rack 6 to 8 inches from the heat source and preheat the oven to broil. Line a baking sheet with aluminum foil.

2 Fill a Dutch oven or other heavy pot with oil to a depth of 1 inch. Heat the oil over medium-high heat to 350°F. Line a wire rack with paper towels, place it on a baking sheet, and set it nearby.

3 Cut the tortillas in half. Carefully add a few tortilla pieces at a time to the oil and fry them, stirring gently, until they're golden and crispy, 2 to 3 minutes. Using a slotted spoon or tongs, transfer the chips to the prepared rack and lightly season them with salt. Repeat with the remaining tortilla pieces.

4 Transfer the tortilla pieces to the foil-lined baking sheet and arrange them in a single layer. Top each piece with 1 tablespoon of the beans, 1 tablespoon of the cheese, and a pinch of salt. Broil just until the cheese has melted, 2 to 3 minutes.

5 Top each nacho with 1 or 2 pickled jalapeños and serve immediately.

Barbacoa FLAUTAS

MAKES 16

Flauta is Spanish for "flute." In Tex-Mex cuisine, a flauta is a tortilla rolled up around a filling like shredded chicken or beef and deep-fried into a crisp finger food that's then usually dipped in guacamole, sour cream, or salsa. They're sometimes called *taquitos* or *tacos dorados*, though *tacos dorados* don't tend to be as tightly rolled. The rolls are often thin, with just a bit of filling, but you also find them folded more loosely around a larger portion of filling and fried until just golden, which is where the term *taco dorado* comes from. I prefer "flauta," but I think it's to distance it from the word *taquito*, which is often used by fast-food joints.

To really be traditional, flautas should be made with corn tortillas. There are some recipes out there that use flour tortillas, but if you ask me, that's not the real deal. Corn tortillas are the only way to go.

Vegetable oil, for softening the tortillas and frying

16 (6-inch) corn tortillas, store-bought or homemade (page 98)

2 cups Braised Beef Barbacoa (page 104)

1 cup shredded Chihuahua cheese

Kosher salt

1 cup Avocado Crema (page 111) or store-bought avocado-tomatillo salsa

TIP

To make chicken flautas, use 2 cups smoked shredded chicken (page 128) or shredded store-bought rotisserie chicken rather than braised beef barbacoa.

1 Fill a Dutch oven or large heavy pot with oil to a depth of ½ inch. Heat the oil over medium-high heat to 350°F.

2 Using tongs, dip a few tortillas at a time into the hot oil until softened, 3 or 4 seconds. Stack them on a plate and cover with a clean kitchen towel to keep warm. Turn off the heat and add enough oil to the pot to raise the depth to 1½ inches. Heat the oil over medium-high heat to 375°F. Line a wire rack with paper towels, place it on a baking sheet, and set it nearby.

3 Put a tortilla on a clean work surface. Spoon 2 tablespoons of the barbacoa down the center of the tortilla, leaving about ½ inch clear around the edges. Sprinkle 1 tablespoon of the cheese over the beef. Fold one side of the tortilla over the filling, then roll up the tortilla to enclose the filling and secure it with a small skewer or toothpick. Repeat to fill the remaining tortillas.

4 Carefully add the flautas, 3 or 4 at a time, to the hot oil and fry, basting them with the oil and occasionally flipping them, until golden brown and crispy, 2½ to 3 minutes. Using a slotted spoon, transfer them to the prepared rack and sprinkle with salt. Repeat to fry the remaining flautas. Let cool slightly, then remove the toothpicks.

5 Serve family-style with avocado crema alongside for dipping.

chiles RELLENOS

THIS DISH was one of the items that just never made the cut when I was ordering Tex-Mex as a kid. The dish always looked so unappetizing to me, but as an adult, I've totally done a one-eighty on the chile relleno. I love the simplicity of it. You have to use a good cheese like queso Oaxaca to get the right texture, especially when it seizes up as it cools. I love the stringy chew that it has. I like to pan-fry it rather than deep-fry it, which gives it a homier spin. Adding a simple chile-and-tomato purée over the top is one of my favorite ways to serve a chile relleno, though you'll also find it served with green sauces or in a walnut cream sauce, which is more authentically Mexican.

FOR THE TOMATO SAUCE

1 (14-ounce) can whole peeled tomatoes

2 small tomatoes, quartered

1 small onion, quartered

1 garlic clove

½ jalapeño pepper, stemmed

1½ teaspoons kosher salt

1½ teaspoons sugar

1½ teaspoons ground cumin

1½ teaspoons dried Mexican oregano

½ teaspoon freshly ground black pepper

FOR THE CHILES

8 small poblano peppers

6 ounces queso fresco, crumbled

6 ounces Oaxaca cheese, shredded

6 ounces Chihuahua cheese, shredded

Vegetable oil, for frying

4 large eggs, separated

1¼ cups all-purpose flour

1 tablespoon kosher salt, plus more to taste

1 tablespoon freshly ground black pepper

TO SERVE

4 ounces queso fresco, crumbled

4 teaspoons chopped fresh cilantro

1 teaspoon dried Mexican oregano

CONTINUES

1 **MAKE THE SAUCE** In a large saucepan set over medium-high heat, combine the canned and fresh tomatoes, onion, garlic, jalapeño, salt, sugar, cumin, oregano, and black pepper. Bring the mixture to a boil. Reduce the heat to medium and simmer until the vegetables are soft, 30 minutes. Using an immersion blender, purée the sauce until smooth. (Alternatively, carefully transfer the sauce to a regular blender, working in batches if necessary, and blend until smooth, then return the sauce to the pot.) If the sauce is too thick, add a little water. Taste and add salt if needed. Keep warm.

2 **PREPARE THE CHILES** Heat a grill to high or heat a grill pan over high heat.

3 Grill the whole poblanos until blackened and blistered on all sides, 3 to 4 minutes per side. (Alternatively, char the chiles poblanos directly on a gas stovetop burner set to medium-high heat, turning them with tongs until blackened and blistered on all sides.) Place the poblanos in a large bowl, cover, and let steam for 15 minutes. Once they're cool enough to handle, peel them and cut a 1-inch slit in the side of each pepper.

4 Combine the cheeses in a medium bowl. Stuff each pepper evenly with the cheese mixture. Set aside.

5 Preheat the oven to 250°F. Place a wire rack on a baking sheet and place the baking sheet in the oven.

6 Fill a Dutch oven or deep cast-iron skillet with oil to a depth of 1½ inches. Heat the oil over medium-high heat to 365°F.

7 In the bowl of a stand mixer fitted with the whisk attachment, beat the egg whites on medium speed until medium-stiff peaks form, about 2 minutes. With the mixer on medium speed, add the egg yolks, one at a time, beating for 20 seconds after each addition. Add ¼ cup of the flour, the salt, and the black pepper and beat for 10 seconds.

8 Transfer the batter to a shallow bowl or dish. Put the remaining 1 cup flour in a separate shallow dish. Dredge the stuffed chiles in the flour, then dip them in the batter to coat, allowing any excess to drip off.

9 Place the chiles in the hot oil, two or three at a time, and cook until they're golden on all sides, about 1½ minutes per side. Using tongs, transfer the chiles to the prepared rack and keep them warm in oven. Repeat to cook the remaining chiles, bringing the oil back to 365°F after each.

10 Place two chiles on each serving plate, top with the sauce, and garnish with the queso fresco, cilantro, and oregano. Serve immediately.

ALBÓNDIGAS

JUST AS THE ITALIANS and Swedes have a meatball-making tradition, so, too, do the Spanish and, by extension, the Mexicans. *Albóndigas* have long been made as a tapas and are typically served with a spicy dipping sauce, but they're also often incorporated into soup, *caldo albóndigas*. I love making just the meatballs, stuffing them with a little nugget of Oaxaca cheese, and cooking them in a rich chile-tomato sauce—the cheese oozes out when you cut into the meatballs. It's a great dish for feeding a lot of people, and they never fail to impress.

FOR THE CHILE SAUCE

2 tablespoons lard
  (see page 24)

1 cup chopped onion

3 garlic cloves

2 cups chicken broth

4 dried ancho chiles,
  stemmed, some seeds
  removed

1½ teaspoons chili powder
  (I like Gebhardt)

¼ teaspoon ground cumin

1 teaspoon kosher salt, plus
  more to taste

FOR THE MEATBALLS

2 tablespoons lard, plus
  melted lard as needed
  for browning

½ cup chopped onion

1 garlic clove

3 (6-inch) corn tortillas,
  store-bought or
  homemade (page 98),
  chopped into small
  pieces

½ cup heavy cream

½ cup Requesón or ricotta
  cheese

1 large egg

2 teaspoons kosher salt

¼ teaspoon dried Mexican
  oregano

½ pound ground sirloin

½ pound ground pork

½ cup cubed Oaxaca cheese
  (about 8 cubes)

TO SERVE

¼ cup coarsely chopped
  fresh cilantro

½ cup sliced radishes

2 serrano peppers, sliced

8 to 12 (6-inch) corn or flour
  tortillas, store-bought
  or homemade (page 98
  or 101)

CONTINUES

1 MAKE THE SAUCE Melt the lard in a medium saucepan set over medium-high heat. Add the onion and garlic and cook, stirring frequently, until the onion is translucent, 3 to 4 minutes. Add the broth, anchos, chili powder, cumin, and salt. Bring to a boil, then reduce the heat to low and simmer until the chiles have softened, 10 minutes. Carefully transfer the mixture to a blender and purée until smooth. Add ¼ cup water and purée to combine. Taste and add salt as needed. Set aside.

2 MAKE THE MEATBALLS Melt the lard in a medium nonstick sauté pan set over medium-high heat. Add the onion and garlic and cook, stirring frequently, until the onion is translucent, 2 to 3 minutes. Add the tortillas and cook, stirring frequently, until the tortillas have softened, 3 to 4 minutes. Transfer the mixture to a food processor and add the cream, Requesón, egg, salt, and oregano. Process until the mixture is smooth and looks like a batter.

3 Put the ground sirloin and the pork in a large bowl and use your hands to combine them well. Add the batter to the meat mixture and use your hands to combine well. Portion the meat mixture into 2-ounce balls, about 8 meatballs.

4 Cut the Oaxaca cheese into as many cubes as there are meatballs. Press a cheese cube into the center of each ball and re-form the meat mixture into a ball, making sure to completely enclose the cheese. Set the meatballs on a baking sheet, cover, and refrigerate for 30 minutes.

5 Preheat the oven to 300°F.

6 Fill a large Dutch oven with melted lard to a depth of ¼ inch. Heat the lard over medium-high heat. When the lard is shimmering, add the meatballs and cook until browned on all sides, about 6 minutes total. Transfer the meatballs to a roasting pan. Roast until dark golden brown, 25 minutes.

7 Drain any fat that has accumulated in the bottom of the roasting pan. Pour the sauce over the meatballs and return them to the oven. Roast until the meatballs are cooked through, 25 to 30 minutes.

8 Serve immediately with cilantro, radishes, serranos, and tortillas alongside.

CAMPECHANA
157

POZOLE WITH SHRIMP & PORK 158

CAMARONES EN AGUA CHILE 161

WEST TEXAS–STYLE STACKED
SHRIMP ENCHILADAS 162

GRILLED OYSTERS DIVORCIADOS 165

WHOLE GRILLED RED SNAPPER WITH
CILANTRO CHIMICHURRI 168

GRILLED SHRIMP DIABLO 171

CEVICHE 172

SHRIMP TACOS DORADOS 175

THE PRESENCE OF Seafood

in Tex-Mex cuisine is directly related to the fact
that Texas sits along the Gulf of Mexico. That said,
seafood didn't have a place on a Tex-Mex menu for a
long time, since the fare evolved in the Rio Grande
Valley and the northern and western parts of the
state. But things have always been different on
the coast. Sure, you'd have all the standard tacos,
enchiladas, and steamy bowls of queso, but seafood
also played a role. This was particularly true in the
likes of Brownsville and Port Isabel, towns located
on the southernmost parts of the coastline; up the
channel islands of South Padre, Corpus Christi, and
Rockport; and on into Houston. (Farther east of
Houston, toward Louisiana, is where Tex-Mex wanes
and Texas-Cajun cuisine takes precedence.) This
chapter shares a few of the best additions to Tex-
Mex courtesy of the Texas Gulf Coast.

DE MARISCOS

SERVES 4

Sort of like a Mexican shrimp cocktail, *campechana* is a far cry from the kind that comes with chilled shrimp alongside a dish of ketchup-y horseradish sauce. It's more of a spicy, vodka-free Bloody-Mary-meets-loads-of-seafood. While *campechana* is often made with just shrimp, I like to use whatever seafood is fresh and in season. I think it's delicious with good ol' saltine crackers, and of course it has to be served in a chilled old-fashioned parfait glass.

4 ounces cleaned squid, tubes and tentacles

1 tablespoon vegetable oil

4 ounces lump crabmeat

4 ounces cooked shrimp

2 avocados, pitted, peeled, and diced

2 cups Campechana Sauce (recipe at right)

Kosher salt

8 to 10 sprigs fresh cilantro

Saltines or tortilla chips, for serving

1 Heat a grill to high or heat a grill pan over high heat.

2 Place the squid and the oil in a small bowl and toss to coat. Grill the squid for 1 minute. Flip and grill until cooked through, 1 to 2 minutes more. Transfer the squid to a cutting board and coarsely chop. Cover and refrigerate until cool.

3 In a medium bowl, combine the chilled squid, crabmeat, shrimp, avocado, and sauce and gently toss to combine. Taste and add salt as needed.

4 Divide among four chilled parfait glasses, garnish with the cilantro, and serve with an iced-tea spoon and saltines or tortilla chips.

CAMPECHANA SAUCE

MAKES 4½ CUPS

¾ cup fresh lime juice

¾ cup ketchup

¾ cup roasted tomato salsa, store-bought or homemade (page 113)

⅓ cup Clamato (clam-tomato juice)

¼ cup Cowboy Gringo Table Hot Sauce (page 112) or store-bought hot sauce, such as Cholula or Tapatío

⅔ cup sliced green olives

1½ cups pico de gallo, store-bought or homemade (page 112)

2 tablespoons dried Mexican oregano

2 teaspoons garlic powder or granulated garlic

1 teaspoon kosher salt

½ teaspoon freshly ground black pepper

In a medium bowl, stir together the lime juice, ketchup, salsa, Clamato juice, hot sauce, olives, pico de gallo, oregano, garlic powder, salt, and pepper.

Serve or store in an airtight container in the refrigerator for up to 3 days.

Pozole
WITH SHRIMP AND PORK

1 pound whole head-on, tail-on large shrimp

½ pound pork shoulder, cut into 1-inch cubes

¼ pound pork belly, skin removed, cut into 1-inch cubes

1 (14.5-ounce) can whole peeled tomatoes

1 cup Standard Chile Paste (page 66)

1½ cups chopped onions

1 cup chopped fresh tomatillos

1 cup chopped poblano pepper

½ cup chopped celery

1 tablespoon chicken bouillon

1 tablespoon dried Mexican oregano

1 tablespoon kosher salt, plus more to taste

2 teaspoons ground cumin

1 bay leaf

1 (15-ounce) can hominy, drained and rinsed

¼ cup chopped fresh cilantro

2 serrano peppers, stemmed and sliced

2 cups shaved green cabbage

½ cup shaved radishes

4 to 6 lime wedges

SERVES 4 OR 5

With deep roots in Mexican culture, pozole hasn't always been a Tex-Mex menu staple, but among the kitchen staff, it has long had a place at restaurant family meals. *Pozole*, another word for "hominy," is a brothy stew with corn as its star. The pork and shrimp simply help amplify the flavor. You'll find any number of garnishes with pozole, from shredded cabbage and serrano peppers to radishes, avocado, and lime.

Now, we got a little fancy when taking the photo for this dish. The picture shows the heads on the shrimp, which looks nice, but it's much easier to enjoy the soup if you remove the heads and shells (and put them to use in the broth) and use only the shrimp meat for the pozole.

1 Remove the heads, tails, and shells from the shrimp and set the peeled shrimp aside.

2 In a large pot over medium-high heat, combine the shrimp heads, tails, and shells and 3 cups water. Cover and bring just to a boil. Reduce the heat to low and simmer, stirring occasionally to release more flavor from the shells, until the shells become reddish orange, about 30 minutes.

3 Meanwhile, split the shrimp in half by running a paring knife down the back from tip to tip and remove the vein. Put the shrimp on a plate, cover, and refrigerate until ready to use.

4 Using a spider or slotted spoon, remove the heads, tails, and shells from the broth and discard them. Add the pork shoulder, pork belly, tomatoes, chile paste, 1 cup of the onions, the tomatillos, poblano, celery, bouillon, oregano, salt, cumin, and bay leaf to the broth. Increase the heat to medium-high and bring the broth to a simmer. Reduce the heat to maintain a low simmer and cook until the pork is tender, about 1 hour.

5 Using a slotted spoon, transfer the pieces of pork to a bowl. Remove the bay leaf. Using an immersion blender, purée the broth mixture until smooth, 3 to 4 minutes. (Alternatively, carefully transfer the broth mixture to a regular blender and purée until smooth, then return it to the pot.) Return the pork to the liquid and add the hominy. Cook over medium-high heat until the hominy is heated through, 10 to 15 minutes. Add the shrimp and cook until the shrimp are light pink and cooked through, about 2 minutes.

6 Serve family-style with the cilantro, serranos, cabbage, remaining onion, radishes, and lime alongside.

CAMARONES
EN AGUA CHILE

SERVES 4

This dish is on the lighter side of the spectrum and uses a milder chile, cucumber, avocado, and lime to highlight the more delicate flavors of the shrimp. The citrus and chiles essentially cure, or "cook," the shrimp, just as in a ceviche, and the result is really bright and refreshing. It's not too complex but is still full of flavor. Enjoy it with an ice-cold Corona.

FOR THE SHRIMP

16 raw large shrimp, peeled, deveined, and butterflied

1 cup fresh lime juice

2 tablespoons kosher salt

FOR THE CHILE WATER

¼ cup fresh lime juice

¾ pound fresh tomatillos, husks removed

½ cup fresh cilantro leaves

¼ cup finely chopped onion

1 serrano pepper

1 teaspoon minced garlic

1 tablespoon kosher salt

TO SERVE

½ cup sliced cucumber

2 avocados, pitted, peeled, and sliced

¼ cup sliced radishes

¼ cup fresh cilantro leaves

¼ cup Cilantro Chimichurri (recipe at right)

1 PREPARE THE SHRIMP In a medium bowl, stir together the shrimp, lime juice, and salt. Cover and refrigerate for 45 minutes to cure the shrimp. Drain the shrimp, cover, and refrigerate until ready to use.

2 MAKE THE CHILE WATER In a food processor or blender, combine the lime juice, tomatillos, cilantro, onion, serrano, garlic, and salt and purée until very smooth, 2 to 3 minutes. Pour the mixture through a fine-mesh strainer, cover, and refrigerate for at least 2 hours or until ready to use.

3 TO SERVE Place four serving bowls in the freezer 15 to 20 minutes before ready to serve. Divide the shrimp evenly among the four chilled bowls. Ladle the cold chile water over the shrimp. Garnish with the cucumber, avocado, radishes, and cilantro, drizzle with the chimichurri, and serve.

MAKES 1½ CUPS

CILANTRO CHIMICHURRI

2 bunches cilantro, tough stems removed

1 serrano pepper, stemmed and coarsely chopped

1 garlic clove

1 teaspoon kosher salt, plus more to taste

1 cup vegetable oil

In a food processor, combine the cilantro, serrano, garlic, and salt and pulse to break down the ingredients. With the processor running, slowly drizzle in the oil and process until well combined, 1 to 2 minutes. Taste and add more salt as needed.

Serve or store in an airtight container in the refrigerator for 2 to 3 days.

WEST TEXAS-STYLE STACKED SHRIMP ENCHILADAS

SERVES 4

YOU MAY NOT REALIZE that not all enchiladas are rolled. In fact, in West Texas and on throughout New Mexico, you also find them stacked, with layers of filling between tortillas similar to Italian lasagne. The original stacked enchiladas were a celebration of the chili sauce into which the tortillas were dipped, with only cheese and chopped onions sprinkled in between them. But over time, the fillings became more varied to include anything from shredded chicken to sautéed spinach and mushrooms. Personally, I like the briny flavor and tender texture of shrimp layered into the mix.

Vegetable oil

12 (6-inch) corn tortillas, store-bought or homemade (page 98)

3 garlic cloves, sliced

⅓ cup chopped onion plus ¼ cup sliced onion

1 jalapeño pepper, stemmed and coarsely chopped

1 teaspoon kosher salt, plus more to taste

½ teaspoon ground cumin

Pinch of ground cloves

1 (14.5-ounce) can whole peeled tomatoes

½ cup Standard Chile Paste (page 66)

½ teaspoon chicken bouillon

1 pound raw large shrimp, peeled (tails removed) and deveined

½ cup chopped fresh cilantro

1½ cups grated Chihuahua cheese

1 avocado, pitted, peeled, and sliced

Avocado oil (optional)

CONTINUES

1 Place an oven rack 6 to 8 inches from the heat source and preheat the oven to broil.

2 Fill a Dutch oven or large heavy pot with oil to a depth of ½ inch. Heat the oil over medium-high heat to 350°F.

3 Using tongs, dip a few tortillas at a time into the hot oil until softened, 3 or 4 seconds. Stack them on a plate and cover with a clean kitchen towel to keep warm.

4 Heat 1 tablespoon oil in a large saucepan set over medium-high heat. When the oil shimmers, add the garlic, chopped onion, jalapeño, salt, cumin, and cloves and cook, stirring frequently, until the onion is translucent, 3 to 4 minutes. Stir in the tomatoes, chile paste, bouillon, and ½ cup water. Bring to a simmer and cook, stirring occasionally, until the ingredients are well integrated and begin to reduce, 3 to 4 minutes. Remove the pan from the heat and, using an immersion blender, purée until smooth. (Alternatively, carefully transfer the mixture to a regular blender and purée until smooth.)

5 In a food processor, pulse the shrimp until coarsely ground, five or six times. Add the shrimp to the sauce and put the pan over medium-low heat. Cook, stirring frequently, until the shrimp are light pink and just cooked through, 4 to 5 minutes. Remove the pan from the heat and stir in ¼ cup of the cilantro to combine. Cover to keep warm.

6 To build the stacked enchiladas, spoon 2 tablespoons of the shrimp sauce over the bottom of an oven-safe bowl or cazuela (see page 22). Cover with a softened tortilla and top with ¼ cup of the shrimp sauce and 2 tablespoons of the cheese. Repeat two more times to create three layers total. Repeat the layering process in three additional bowls with the remaining ingredients.

7 Place the bowls on a baking sheet. Broil just until the cheese melts, 2 to 3 minutes.

8 Serve immediately with the avocado, sliced onion, and remaining cilantro alongside. Drizzle with avocado oil, if desired.

GRILLED oysters DIVORCIADOS

SERVES 8

THERE'S NO DENYING the deliciousness of a simple raw oyster. But grilled oysters are fantastic, and they're my go-to whenever I find some good ones in season. I love serving a big platter of them just off the grill and still bubbling. You may be tempted to make either the Cilantro Chimichurri Butter or the Chile de Árbol Butter instead of both—don't! They work so well together, and alternating between the two at the table is a big part of the fun.

I've specified that you use a charcoal grill for this recipe, and I mean it. What makes grilled oysters so irresistible is the smokiness that scents their briny flavor. You just can't get that from a gas grill.

24 raw oysters

½ cup Chile de Árbol Butter (recipe follows)

½ cup Cilantro Chimichurri Butter (recipe follows)

Rock salt

12 lime wedges

1 Heat a charcoal grill to high.

2 Clean the outside of the oysters under running water to remove excess dirt and grit. Hold one oyster in a thick towel with the hinge side sticking out. Insert the tip of an oyster knife under the hinge and twist until the top shell lifts away. While holding the oyster level, so as not to allow the liquor inside to spill, slide the tip of the knife around the edge of the shell. Use the knife to detach the muscle from the top shell and pull the shells apart. Remove the top shell. Wipe away any dirt or grit that is inside. Use the knife and flip the oyster, detaching it from the shell. Place the oysters in their half shells on a baking sheet and keep them level.

3 Top 12 of the oysters with 1 teaspoon of Chile de Árbol Butter each and the remaining 12 oysters with 1 teaspoon of the Cilantro Chimichurri Butter each. Set the oysters on the grill grate directly over the fire, making sure they sit level so their juices and the butters don't run out.

4 Cover the grill and cook until the oysters plump and the butter is melted and bubbling, 2 to 3 minutes. Transfer the oysters to a serving platter lined with rock salt.

5 Serve family-style with the lime wedges on the side.

CONTINUES

CHILE DE ÁRBOL BUTTER

MAKES ABOUT 1/2 CUP

⅓ cup unsalted butter, at room
   temperature

2 tablespoons Super-Spicy "Staff Only"
   Salsa (page 116) or store-bought hot
   sauce

Place the butter and salsa in a small
bowl. Whisk to combine.

The butter will keep in an airtight
container in the refrigerator for up to
3 days.

MAKES ABOUT 1/2 CUP

CILANTRO CHIMICHURRI BUTTER

⅓ cup butter, at room temperature

2 tablespoons Cilantro Chimichurri
   (page 161)

Place the butter and chimichurri in a
small bowl. Whisk to combine.

The butter will keep in an airtight
container in the refrigerator for up to
3 days.

Whole Grilled RED SNAPPER

SERVES 4

WITH CILANTRO CHIMICHURRI

Whole grilled fish is coastal Tex-Mex at its finest. I love the char and smokiness a wood-fired grill brings to fish, and the taste of salt water that sizzles into the flesh. I typically don't like messing with whole fish when eating, but this is a worthy exception. It helps to score the skin every inch or so before cooking, which makes it easier to break off a good piece without the bones. It also creates more surfaces and edges to char and get crispy.

1 (1¼- to 2-pound) whole red snapper, gutted and scaled

1½ cups Cilantro Chimichurri (page 161)

2 limes, quartered

Sea salt

1 Heat a grill to high.

2 Rinse the snapper and pat dry. Use a sharp knife to score the fish on an angle every inch, making three or four slits on each side. Rub the fish with ¾ cup of the chimichurri, making sure to get the sauce into all the slits.

3 Place the fish in a grilling basket and clamp to hold the fish securely. Grill the fish until the meat begins to pull away from the bones, 5 to 6 minutes per side.

4 Serve the whole fish family-style with the remaining chimichurri, lime wedges, and salt alongside.

If you can't find red snapper, try pompano, black bass, or branzino.

GRILLED SHRIMP DIABLO

IT'S NO SECRET that I love shrimp, and I also truly love all things *hot*, as in spicy. Therefore, this dish is absolutely a favorite. The term *diablo*, or "devil," indicates that these shrimp have some fire in them—the chile paste really brings the heat. They're a little messy to eat, but worth the effort.

A charcoal grill is a must here, because the smokiness it imparts is necessary for the full effect. Normally you don't want any flames to leap up from the fire and possibly burn whatever you're cooking, but for this dish, a little singeing is a great thing. Be careful not to grill the shrimp too long, or they'll become tough.

SERVES 4

12 large head-on, shell-on shrimp

1 cup Standard Chile Paste (page 66)

¾ cup vegetable oil

⅓ cup fresh lime juice

1 tablespoon chicken bouillon

1 bunch cilantro, tough stems removed

2 garlic cloves

2 limes, halved

1 Leaving the shells on, cut down the center of the back of each shrimp with a paring knife, remove the vein, and butterfly them. Place the shrimp in a large bowl and set aside.

2 In a blender, combine the chile paste, oil, lime juice, bouillon, cilantro, and garlic and purée until smooth, about 1 minute. Pour 1 cup of the sauce into the bowl with the shrimp and toss to combine. Cover and refrigerate for 30 minutes. Pour the remaining sauce into a large bowl, cover, and set aside.

3 Heat a charcoal grill to high.

4 Place the shrimp flesh-side down on the hot grill and cook until charred, 1 to 2 minutes. Using tongs, turn the shrimp over and cook until charred on the outside and cooked through, 1 minute more. Transfer the grilled shrimp to the bowl with the remaining marinade and toss to combine.

5 Squeeze the limes over the shrimp and serve family-style.

C E V I C H E

Ceviche is a longtime favorite of mine. You don't find it on a lot of Tex-Mex menus unless you're along the coast, where it's one of the easiest ways to enjoy super-fresh seafood. This recipe is a perfect "all-purpose" ceviche that you can make using any fish, shrimp, scallops, or whatever you prefer. When it comes to fish and shellfish, I am a big fan of Gulf snapper, flounder, Nantucket Bay scallops, and—most of all—Santa Barbara spot prawns.

SERVES 4 AS AN APPETIZER

½ pound boneless, skinless red snapper

5 tablespoons fresh lime juice

3 tablespoons Cilantro Chimichurri (page 161)

1 tablespoon fresh orange juice

1 tablespoon olive oil

1 tablespoon finely chopped onion

1½ teaspoons kosher salt, plus more to taste

2 tablespoons thinly sliced radish

6 sprigs fresh cilantro

½ avocado, pitted, peeled, and sliced

4 lime wedges

1 Cut the fish into ¼-inch cubes and put them in a small bowl. Pour 4 tablespoons of the lime juice over the fish and gently stir to combine. Cover the fish with plastic wrap, pressing it directly against the surface of the fish to eliminate any air contact, and refrigerate for 20 minutes.

2 Drain the juice from fish. Add the remaining 1 tablespoon lime juice, the chimichurri, orange juice, oil, onion, and salt and stir to combine.

3 Serve ice-cold with radishes, cilantro, avocado, and lime wedges alongside.

THE
FISH TACO

It's true—fish tacos are not Tex-Mex. They come from the 800-mile stretch of Mexican coastline known as Baja. Not surprisingly, seafood features prominently in the region's coastal cuisine, influenced heavily by native ingredients such as chiles, cilantro, Mexican oregano, and corn, as well as the Spanish culinary traditions from the early missions of the seventeenth century.

It's commonly believed that Japanese fishermen who trawled the waters of Baja before World War II introduced their tempura cooking techniques to the region. By the 1950s, tempura-fried fish had found its way into tortillas and out to the masses thanks to industrious street vendors. The Baja townships of Ensenada and San Felipe both lay claim to inventing the fish taco.

In the 1970s, Southern California surfers found the fast, fresh, easy-to-eat fish taco to be a satiating snack while hunting for the perfect wave. One such surfer, Ralph Rubio, is credited with bringing the fish taco to the masses in California. In 1983, he launched Rubio's Fresh Mexican Grill, now Rubio's Coastal Grill, which now has 160 locations in California and throughout the Southwest.

The original fish taco featured corn tortillas, a few morsels of fried (not grilled) fish, some fresh cabbage, and a dollop of spicy mayo. It was the perfect package of texture and flavor—crispy with creamy, savory with sweet—and could usually be finished in two or three bites (finger licking encouraged). The fish was usually wahoo, marlin, or yellowtail, all of which are native to Baja—not the tilapia, catfish, or other mild white fish we typically see throughout America today.

It's highly likely that some sort of fresh catch from the Gulf of Mexico along the Texas and Mexico borders was cooked up and wrapped in a tortilla as well. But having tasted the real deal along the shorelines of Baja for myself, I'm more than happy to let the region claim the fish taco as its own creation.

SHRIMP TACOS DORADOS

TACOS DORADOS is simply another form of flauta or *taquito*, only they are not rolled as tightly into a fluted shape. They tend to be a little wider, like a street taco, gently rolled and quickly fried. The word *dorado* means "golden," thus giving you a clue that these tacos are fried. Most flautas are filled with cheese and a meat such as shredded chicken or beef, but I think making these tacos with large, plump shrimp is a delicious alternative.

Vegetable oil, for softening tortillas

8 (6-inch) corn tortillas, store-bought or homemade (page 98)

1 pound raw large shrimp, peeled (tails removed) and deveined

1 tablespoon finely chopped onion

1 tablespoon finely chopped jalapeño pepper

5 tablespoons chopped fresh cilantro

½ teaspoon kosher salt, plus more to taste

8 teaspoons shredded Chihuahua, Monterey Jack, or Oaxaca cheese

1 avocado, pitted, peeled, and sliced

1 cup shredded cabbage

½ cup roasted tomato salsa, store-bought or homemade (page 113)

Lime wedges

1 Fill a Dutch oven or large heavy pot with oil to a depth of ½ inch. Heat the oil over medium-high heat to 350°F.

2 Using tongs, dip a few tortillas at a time into the hot oil until softened, 3 or 4 seconds. Stack them on a plate and cover with a clean kitchen towel to keep warm. Leave the oil in the pot but turn off the heat.

3 In a food processor, pulse the shrimp until coarsely chopped, five or six times. Transfer the shrimp to a medium bowl and add the onion, jalapeño, 1 tablespoon of the cilantro, and the salt.

4 Lay the softened tortillas on a clean work surface and divide the shrimp mixture evenly among them. Spread the shrimp over half of each tortilla, leaving ¼ inch around the edges. Top each with 1 teaspoon of the cheese, fold the tortilla over the filling, and press well to seal.

5 Return the oil to 375°F over medium-high heat. Line a wire rack with paper towels, place it on a baking sheet, and set it nearby.

6 Gently place the dorados in the oil, a few at a time, and cook until the tortilla is lightly golden brown and crispy and the shrimp are cooked through, 2 to 3 minutes per side. Transfer the dorados to the prepared rack and sprinkle with salt. Repeat to fry the remaining dorados.

7 Serve family-style with the avocado, cabbage, remaining cilantro, salsa, and lime wedges alongside.

AL CAR-BÓN

TO THE COALS

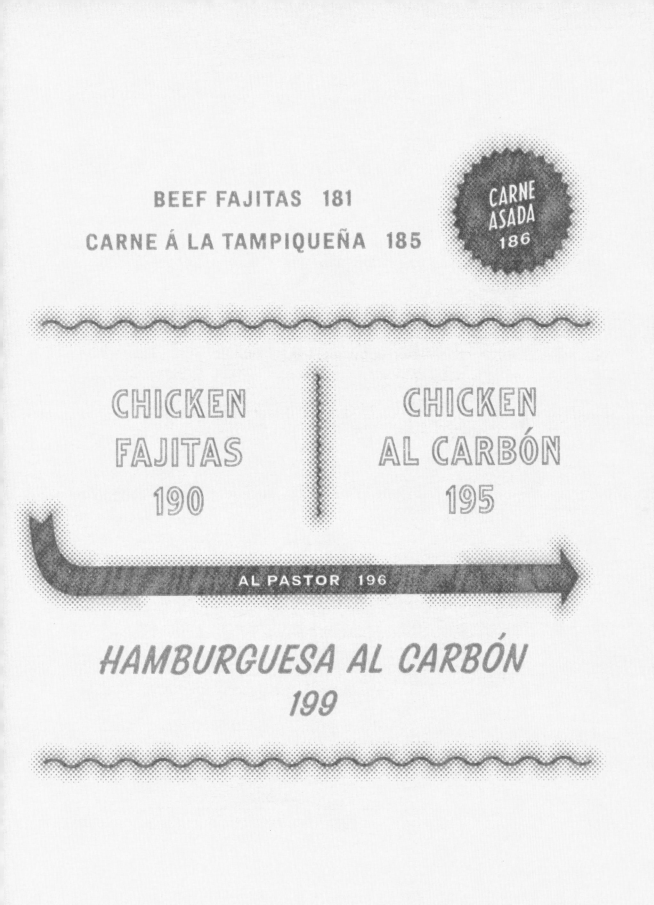

BEEF FAJITAS 181

CARNE Á LA TAMPIQUEÑA 185

CARNE ASADA 186

CHICKEN FAJITAS 190

CHICKEN AL CARBÓN 195

AL PASTOR 196

HAMBURGUESA AL CARBÓN 199

Charcoal or WOOD-FIRED GRILL COOKING

(as it pertains to Tex-Mex) dates to the early Aztec and Mayan cultures and is still a significant part of Mexican cuisines today. In Mexico, you'll commonly see street or market vendors selling meats *al carbón*, and people can take home a whole chicken, hamburgers, or cuts of beef, pork, or lamb to share with their family.

All the recipes in this chapter rely on a charcoal or wood-fired grill. That's just the way it is, since you can't get the necessary smoky flavor from a gas grill. So before you proceed, go ahead and stock up on charcoal, get the grill ready, and prepare to just commit! I promise it's worth it.

BEEF Fajitas

SERVES 4 to 6

THE BIGGEST MISTAKE people make with beef fajitas is using too much citrus in the marinade—and then marinating the meat for way too long. The acid in lime juice cooks the meat, often resulting in a texture that is dry and gritty. My not-so-secret weapon for my fajita marinade is canned pineapple juice. Pineapple contains an enzyme that tenderizes the meat without cooking it. And, bonus, the canned juice has added sugar in it, which helps caramelize the surface of the fajitas as they cook on the grill. Save the lime juice to squeeze on the fajitas once they're cooked.

FOR THE BEEF

2 pounds outside skirt steak (see page 193), trimmed

½ cup canned pineapple juice

¼ cup soy sauce

2 tablespoons vegetable oil

2 tablespoons dry white wine

1 tablespoon Standard Chile Paste (page 66)

¼ cup packed light brown sugar

¼ onion, sliced

1 garlic clove, minced

Generous pinch of freshly ground black pepper

FOR THE VEGETABLES

2 tablespoons vegetable oil

1 onion, sliced

1 large poblano pepper

TO SERVE

8 to 10 (6-inch) flour tortillas, store-bought or homemade (page 101)

Foamy Butter (recipe follows)

2 cups chopped lettuce

2 cups shredded cheddar cheese

1 cup pico de gallo, store-bought or homemade (page 112)

2 cups guacamole, store-bought or homemade (page 68)

1 cup sour cream

1 PREPARE THE MEAT Place the steak in a large resealable plastic bag. Add the pineapple juice, soy sauce, oil, wine, chile paste, brown sugar, onion, garlic, and black pepper. Remove as much air as possible from the bag and seal. Move the steak around to evenly coat it in the marinade. Refrigerate for 4 hours and up to 24 hours, moving the steak around four or five times to evenly distribute the marinade.

2 Heat a grill to high.

3 Remove the steak from the marinade and pat dry (discard the marinade). Grill the steak for 4 minutes per side, or until the internal temperature reaches 125°F. Transfer the steak to a plate and let it rest for 5 to 10 minutes. (Keep the grill hot.) Thinly slice the meat at an angle against the grain. Cover to keep warm.

4 PREPARE THE VEGETABLES Heat the oil in a medium sauté pan set over medium-high heat. When the oil shimmers, add the onion and cook, stirring frequently, just until it begins to lightly brown, 2 to 3 minutes. Reduce the heat to low, cover, and cook until the onion is tender, 4 to 5 inutes. Cover to keep warm.

5 Grill the poblano pepper whole just until it's charred on each side, 3 to 4 minutes. Remove the stem and seeds and slice the pepper into wide strips. Cover to keep warm.

6 Wrap the tortillas in aluminum foil. Put them on the grill to warm them through, 2 to 3 minutes.

7 Transfer the onion and pepper to a plate and top with the steak. Serve family-style with a side dish of the butter, lettuce, cheese, sour cream, pico de gallo, and guacamole, and the warm tortillas alongside.

FOAMY BUTTER

MAKES 1 CUP

2 garlic cloves, grated

2 teaspoons chicken bouillon

¼ cup dry white wine

½ cup (1 stick) unsalted butter, at room temperature

½ cup (1 stick) margarine, at room temperature

In a small bowl, combine the garlic, bouillon, and wine.

In the bowl of a stand mixer fitted with the whisk attachment, combine the butter and margarine and beat on high speed until light and fluffy, about 5 minutes. Stop to scrape down the sides of the bowl as needed. With the mixer on low speed, gradually add the wine mixture. Increase the speed to high and beat until the mixture is light and airy, about 5 minutes.

Fill a medium saucepan with water to a depth of 2 inches. Bring the water to a boil over hight heat. Reduce the heat to maintain a simmer.

Place the bowl of butter over the simmering water and leave it until the mixture is foamy and melted, about 5 minutes. Pour the butter into a small serving dish to serve with the fajitas.

TIP

It's important to use both butter and margarine to get the "just right" foamy effect.

YOU MUST
MESQUITE

For an authentic Tex-Mex flavor, the best and only wood to use for grilling is mesquite. This hardwood grills really hot and fast, and imparts a distinctive smokiness to foods that fruit woods and oak just don't achieve. However, using it for smoking meats over a long period of time can impart a bitter, acrid taste that isn't desirable, so it's not a good choice for barbecue.

Mesquite has been the grilling wood of choice in South and West Texas for more than a century. At one point in time, it was the only source of wood that could be found in the South Texas Valley. But that wasn't always the case. Prior to the mid-nineteenth century, the region was a verdant grassland where buffalo roamed free. But with the growth of cattle ranching throughout the southern and western part of the state, overgrazing devastated the prairies, leaving scrub brush and thorny mesquite trees to take root in place of the grasses. Mesquite wood became the only fuel for campfire cooking, which, over the course of the past century, led to the unique flavors in Tex-Mex cuisine.

CARNE À LA TAMPIQUEÑA

SERVES 4

This dish gets its name from the port of Tampico in the Mexican state of Tamaulipas (its name means "little Tampico"). It's traditionally served as one whole skirt steak—rather than cut into strips, as with fajitas—but some restaurants opt to showcase a nicer cut of meat such as tenderloin.

While the steak and its preparation are important, what makes a dish a *tampiqueña* is its presentation. On an oval platter, the steak is always served with cheese enchiladas (see page 124, usually with mole sauce instead of chili gravy), guacamole (see page 68), and refried beans (see page 61). When cooking this style of meat, I highly recommend keeping with tradition and serving the appropriate sides on the plate as I've described. Something about letting their flavors exist together on one dish makes the steak taste even better.

1 (1½-pound) piece center-cut beef tenderloin

¼ cup packed light brown sugar

1 garlic clove, minced

¼ small onion, cut into matchsticks

¼ cup soy sauce

1 tablespoon Standard Chile Paste (page 66)

2 tablespoons dry white wine

Zest and juice of 1 orange

2 tablespoons vegetable oil

1 teaspoon kosher salt, plus more to taste

Generous pinch of freshly ground black pepper

Maldon salt, for finishing

1 Place the meat in a large resealable plastic bag. Add the brown sugar, garlic, onion, soy sauce, chile paste, wine, orange zest, orange juice, oil, salt, and pepper. Remove as much air as possible from the bag and seal. Move the steak around to evenly coat it in the marinade. Refrigerate for 4 hours and up to 24 hours, moving the steak around four or five times to evenly distribute the marinade.

2 Heat a charcoal grill to high. (If using gas, place the gauge on the highest heat possible.)

3 Remove the meat from the marinade and pat dry (discard the marinade). Season with kosher salt. Grill until charred on both sides, 2 to 3 minutes per side, or until the internal temperature reaches 115°F. Transfer the meat to a plate, cover, and let rest for 5 minutes. Season with Maldon salt and serve immediately.

CARNE ASADA

A slightly simpler version of fajitas (page 181), *carne asada*, or "grilled beef," isn't served with all the accompaniments (shredded lettuce, guacamole, etc.). Instead, it is served as juicy cuts of grilled meat rolled in fresh flour tortillas, sometimes with grilled onions but rarely anything else. You sometimes find it on a Tex-Mex menu as *tacos al carbón*, fajita tacos, or simply *carne asada*. The simplicity of the tender meat combined with a soft, fluffy tortilla is magical.

SERVES 4

1 pound rib eye cap, rib eye steak, or skirt steak

¼ cup soy sauce

2 tablespoons vegetable oil

2 tablespoons white wine

¼ cup packed light brown sugar

1 tablespoon Standard Chile Paste (page 66)

Zest and juice of 1 orange

¼ small onion, cut into matchsticks

1 garlic clove, minced

Generous pinch of freshly ground black pepper

8 (6-inch) flour tortillas, store-bought or homemade (page 101)

1 teaspoon kosher salt, plus more to taste

Maldon salt, for finishing

1 Place the steak in a large resealable plastic bag. Add the soy sauce, oil, wine, brown sugar, chile paste, orange zest, orange juice, onion, garlic, and pepper. Remove as much air as possible from the bag and seal. Move the steak around to evenly coat it in the marinade. Refrigerate for 4 hours and up to 24 hours, moving the steak four or five times to evenly distribute the marinade.

2 Heat a charcoal grill to high. (If using gas, place the gauge on the highest heat possible.)

3 Wrap the tortillas in aluminum foil. Put them on the grill to warm them through, 2 to 3 minutes.

4 Remove the meat from the marinade and pat dry (discard the marinade). Season with the kosher salt. Grill until charred on both sides, 2 to 3 minutes per side, or until the internal temperature reaches 125°F. Transfer the steak to a cutting board, cover, and let rest for 5 minutes. Thinly slice the steak and season it with Maldon salt, if desired. Serve with the warm tortillas.

MEAT CUT

The challenge with fajita meat is that the hands-down best cut to use—the outside skirt—is largely unavailable to the general public. In fact, more than 90 percent of it is shipped to Japan, where buyers are willing to pay a higher price for it than they are in the United States. The rest is sold to restaurants, which can purchase it through American meat packers or even import it from Mexico. When aged properly, outside skirt doesn't even need to be tenderized; it's great as is. So if you know a good butcher, walk in, get on your knees, and flat out beg him to bring it in for you!

For most home cooks, the inside skirt is the cut you'll likely see at the market. It's a less tender, chewier part of the diaphragm, hence the need to marinate and tenderize. Most skirt steaks come rolled up by the butcher and trimmed slightly. If you have the time to be selective, ask to see the cut unrolled before you buy it and make sure there aren't parts that have been trimmed too thin and that the meat has not been cut into separate pieces. One large skirt is about two feet long and should have a fairly consistent thickness all the way across. If this is not the case, you can always split it where it noticeably gets thinner and cook the thicker section a little longer.

If you can't get good skirt steak, the next-best options are well-marbled tender cuts such as flat-iron steak, hanger steak (butterflied), or sirloin flap. Ask your butcher if the selections have been wet-aged at all, which will help contribute to the overall tenderness of the meat.

SERVES 4

FOR THE CHICKEN

11 garlic cloves

2 teaspoons dried Mexican oregano

2 bay leaves

½ cup kosher salt

2 pounds boneless, skinless chicken breasts (see Tip)

¼ cup soy sauce

½ cup canned pineapple juice

2 tablespoons vegetable oil

2 tablespoons white wine

¼ onion, sliced

¼ cup packed light brown sugar

1 tablespoon Standard Chile Paste (page 66)

Generous pinch of freshly ground black pepper

Chicken fajitas sort of rode the coattails of the beef fajita trend in the 1980s and '90s. To me they've always been a distant second to beef, but the one place that has a serious edge on the chicken fajita game was Little Pappasito's Cantina in Houston. They served the grilled vegetables and chicken on a hot skillet, with a little metal dish of frothy melted garlic butter on the side. You pour a little of the butter over everything before enclosing it all in a flour tortilla. It completely negated the idea that you were eating healthier by ordering chicken, but it took the fajita taco to a whole other gluttonous level.

1 **MAKE THE CHICKEN** Bring 2 cups water to a boil in a small saucepan set over high heat. Remove the pan from the heat and add 10 of the garlic cloves, the oregano, bay leaves, and salt. Stir until the salt has dissolved. Add 1½ quarts ice water and stir to combine. Place the chicken breasts in the brine, making sure they are fully submerged. Cover and refrigerate for 3 hours.

2 Place the chicken in a large resealable plastic bag. Add the remaining garlic clove, the soy sauce, pineapple juice, oil, wine, onion, brown sugar, chile paste, and pepper. Remove as much air as possible from the bag and seal. Refrigerate for 20 to 30 minutes.

3 Heat a grill to high.

4 Remove the chicken from the marinade and pat dry (discard the marinade). Grill until cooked through and the meat reaches an internal temperature of 165°F, 5 to 7 minutes per side. Transfer the chicken to a cutting board, cover, and let rest for 5 to 10 minutes. (Keep the grill hot.) Thinly slice the chicken and keep warm.

fajitas

FOR THE VEGETABLES

2 tablespoons vegetable oil

1 onion, sliced

1 teaspoon kosher salt

1 large poblano pepper

TO SERVE

8 to 10 (6-inch) flour
tortillas, store-bought or
homemade (page 101)

Foamy Butter (page 182)

2 cups chopped lettuce

2 cups shredded cheddar
cheese

1 cup pico de gallo, store-
bought or homemade
(page 112)

2 cups guacamole, store-
bought or homemade
(page 68)

1 cup sour cream

5 PREPARE THE VEGETABLES Heat the oil in a medium sauté pan set over medium-high heat. When the oil shimmers, add the onion and cook, stirring frequently, just until it begins to lightly brown, 2 to 3 minutes. Reduce the heat to low, add ½ teaspoon of the salt, cover, and cook until the onion is tender, 4 to 5 minutes.

6 Grill the poblano over high heat just until charred, 3 to 4 minutes. Remove the stem and seeds and slice into wide strips. Add the remaining ½ teaspoon salt and cover to keep warm.

7 Wrap the tortillas in aluminum foil. Put them on the grill to warm them through, 2 to 3 minutes.

8 Transfer the onion and pepper to a plate and top with the chicken. Serve family-style with a small dish of the foamy butter, a plate of lettuce, cheese, pico de gallo, guacamole, and sour cream, and the warm tortillas alongside.

TIP

Try to avoid the oversize conventional chicken breasts most groceries sell. Opt instead for natural breasts, which, because they are smaller, will cook more evenly. If you can't find them, I suggest gently pounding conventional breasts between plastic wrap to a ¾-inch thickness before you brine and cook the chicken.

THE FAJITA:
AUTHENTICALLY TEX-MEX

A lot of Tex-Mex dishes take this route: they originated in Mexico and evolved to suit Texan—and, by extension, American—taste preferences as they were adopted. But fajitas originated in Texas. There are a number of legends by folks claiming to have invented the fajita—Sonny Falcon, of small-town Kyle, in Central Texas, in 1969; Otilia Garza, of Austin's Roundup Restaurant in South Texas; and Ninfa "Mama" Rodriguez Laurenzo, of Houston's famed Ninfa's on Navigation, to name a few. But the true origin of fajitas can really be traced to the dusty cattle ranches of West Texas. After a hard day's work, Mexican vaqueros were often given a few scraps of meat as part of their payment. Oftentimes those cuts included the head of a cow, the entrails, and other meat trimmings such as skirt steak. From these cuts, the ranch hands would make versions of traditional Mexican *barbacoa*, menudo, and *arracheras*, which later become known as fajitas.

Fajita means "belt" or "sash," which is a pretty accurate description of what the skirt steak looks like before it is sliced into strips after grilling. These days, most beef fajitas are, sadly, made with other cuts, including flap, flank, or even sirloin. You'll also find that a variety of other fajita options have joined the lineup, including chicken, shrimp, and portobello mushroom. The hallmark of all fajitas is their presentation: sizzling on a hot *comal* or skillet with grilled onion and served with a condiment plate of shredded cheese, sour cream, guacamole, and pico de gallo, as well as warm flour tortillas for building your own taco.

There's one clarification I never thought I'd have to make, but living outside of Texas has assured me I do: Fajitas are *not* a stir-fry dish. Cutting up strips of steak and sautéing them in a skillet with onions and peppers is not the way to make fajitas. If this is something you do, it's all good—just call them something else.

Chicken AL CARBÓN

A beautiful and delicious dish, chicken *al carbón* is a whole chicken roasted over the fire. To me, what makes this shine is the extra time it requires to smoke on the grill, which develops a distinctive campfire flavor. The variety of light and dark meat, along with the occasional charred bits of skin, are delicious when rolled up in a tortilla. Served with rice and beans, fresh salsa, and maybe some grilled onions, this is a hands-on family dish, where you pull off the meat and build your own tacos with corn or flour tortillas.

1 (4- to 5-pound) whole chicken, giblets and excess fat removed

1 cup fresh orange juice

Juice of 1 lime

2 tablespoons vegetable oil, plus more for grilling

1½ tablespoons soy sauce

½ (3.5-ounce) packet achiote paste (see Tip)

1 dried ancho chile, stemmed

6 dried chiles de árbol, stemmed

2 garlic cloves

½ teaspoon ground cumin

1 tablespoon kosher salt, plus more to taste

8 (6-inch) flour tortillas, store-bought or homemade (page 101)

2 medium onions, cut into thick rings

3 large jalapeño peppers, stemmed and cut in half lengthwise

TIP You can find achiote paste in the spice section of most grocery stores or online.

1 Place the chicken on a clean work surface, breast-side down. Using kitchen shears, cut lengthwise along both sides of the backbone from the neck to the tail. Remove the backbone and save it for stock or discard. Open the bird like a book, then place it skin-side up. Press down firmly with both hands to flatten the bird.

2 In a blender, combine the orange juice, lime juice, oil, soy sauce, achiote paste, ancho, chiles de árbol, garlic, cumin, and salt and purée until smooth, about 1 minute. Transfer 1 cup of the mixture to a large resealable plastic bag. Reserve the remaining sauce. Add the chicken to the bag and move it around to fully coat it in the sauce. Remove as much air as possible and seal. Refrigerate overnight or for up to 24 hours.

3 Remove the chicken from the refrigerator 1 hour before grilling to come to room temperature.

4 Heat a charcoal grill to 400°F, or until the coals are ash-gray and very hot.

5 Wrap the tortillas in aluminum foil. Put them on the grill to warm them through, 2 to 3 minutes.

6 Place the chicken, breast-side up, on the hot grill and cook until lightly browned, 15 minutes. Flip the chicken and baste the cooked side with the reserved sauce. Grill for 15 minutes more. Flip the chicken and baste again. Grill for 15 minutes more. Flip the chicken, baste with the remaining sauce, and grill until the internal temperature reaches 160°F, about 15 minutes more. Transfer to a cutting board, cover, and let rest for 10 to 15 minutes. (Keep the grill hot.)

7 Meanwhile, lightly brush the onion rings and jalapeños with oil and season with salt. Grill the vegetables until char marks appear and the vegetables begin to soften, 3 to 4 minutes per side.

8 Carve the chicken into 8 pieces and then slice the breasts. Serve family-style with the grilled vegetables and warm tortillas alongside.

½ cup fresh pineapple juice

½ cup white vinegar

¼ cup vegetable oil

½ cup Standard Chile Paste (page 66)

¼ cup achiote paste (see Tip, page 195)

6 tablespoons light brown sugar

4 garlic cloves

1½ teaspoons dried Mexican oregano

1½ teaspoons ground cumin

1½ teaspoons freshly ground black pepper

½ teaspoon ground cinnamon

¼ teaspoon ground cloves

2 tablespoons kosher salt, plus more to taste

IN TEXAS, beef has always been king. Early Tex-Mex menus didn't usually include much pork, if any at all. But its overall significance in authentic Mexican cuisine has led to the addition of various pork dishes on Tex-Mex menus in recent years. From the Spanish word for "shepherd," *pastor* has a direct connection to the Lebanese immigrants who came to Mexico City in the early twentieth century and brought shawarma with them. *Al pastor* is typically made from a marinated, thin-sliced pork shoulder that is stacked onto a *trompo* grill and carved off the spit. Obviously most folks won't do all that at home, so my recipe is adapted for a backyard grill. As a complement to the pineapple juice in the marinade, the dish is typically served with some sort of pineapple condiment, and in corn tortillas.

1 In a blender, combine the pineapple juice, vinegar, oil, chile paste, achiote paste, brown sugar, garlic, oregano, cumin, pepper, cinnamon, cloves, and salt and purée until smooth, about 1 minute. Place the sliced pork into a large resealable plastic bag and pour half the sauce over it. Reserve the remaining sauce. Remove as much air as possible from the bag and seal. Move the pork around to evenly coat it in the marinade. Refrigerate overnight or for up to 24 hours, massaging the meat occasionally to work in the marinade.

1 (2½- to 3-pound) boneless pork shoulder, cut into ¼-inch-thick slices

12 (6-inch) corn tortillas, store-bought or homemade (page 98), warmed

½ small pineapple, peeled, cored, and cut into ½-inch-thick wedges

1 small onion, chopped

Chopped fresh cilantro, for serving

Radish slices, for serving

Lime wedges, for serving

2 Pour the remaining sauce into a small saucepan set over medium-high heat. Bring to a simmer and cook, stirring occasionally, until reduced by half, about 5 minutes. Transfer the sauce to an airtight container and refrigerate until ready to use. Reheat on the stovetop before using.

3 Heat a charcoal grill to high, or until the coals are ash-gray and very hot.

4 Wrap the tortillas in aluminum foil. Put them on the grill to warm them through, 2 to 3 minutes.

5 Remove the pork from the marinade and pat dry (discard the marinade). Grill the pork until it reaches an internal temperature of 145°F and is slightly charred around the edges, 4 to 5 minutes per side. Transfer the pork to a plate, cover, and keep warm. (Keep the grill hot.)

6 Grill the pineapple wedges until charred on both sides, 4 to 5 minutes per side. Chop the pineapple into bite-size pieces.

7 To serve, place some of the pork on a tortilla and top it with some grilled pineapple, onion, cilantro, radishes, and sauce. Serve with lime wedges.

HAMBURGUESA AL CARBÓN

SERVES 4

FOR AS LONG AS THERE HAVE BEEN Tex-Mex restaurants, there have been kids who insist they want a hamburger instead of whatever goodness awaits on the menu. Luckily for them, most restaurants have long been happy to accommodate. Of course, the kid versions usually arrive as dry, well-done patties with a slice of melted cheddar on your average white bun. But I believe in taking a little pride in making a burger. I prefer a single 8-ounce patty (70% lean ground beef is preferable), loosely packed so the burger doesn't get too dense while it's cooking. I top it like a standard American burger—with mustard, American cheese, shredded lettuce, pickles, and onion—with one addition. Before you top it with a bun, pour a little chili gravy over the patty. It makes things a little messier, but who really cares? It tastes so good!

2 pounds ground beef (preferably 70% lean)

Kosher salt

8 slices American cheese

Unsalted butter

4 (5-inch) hamburger buns

Yellow mustard

¼ cup finely chopped onion

Dill pickle slices

½ cup Chili Gravy (page 125), hot, or store-bought salsa

1 cup shredded lettuce

4 slices tomato (if in season)

TIP If you don't have a grill, you can achieve the same burger greatness on a griddle. Divide each patty into two patties. Get them nice and flat. Cook them on the griddle until the meat is no longer pink halfway up the side of the patty, 3 minutes. Flip and place one slice of cheese on each patty. Cook for 2 minutes more for medium doneness. From there, build a classic double burger.

1 Divide the ground beef into four 8-ounce balls. One at a time, place the balls between two pieces of plastic wrap and flatten them with the bottom of a cast-iron skillet or other heavy pot until the patty is about 6 inches in diameter. Cover and refrigerate the patties for at least 30 minutes and up to overnight.

2 Heat a charcoal grill to 400°F, or until the coals are ash-gray and very hot.

3 Generously season each patty with salt. Place the patties on the grill and cook until medium inside with a browning crust on the edges, 3 to 4 minutes per side, rotating them a quarter turn halfway through cooking on each side. When you flip the patties, top each with 2 slices of American cheese. Let the cheese melt for about 2 minutes before rotating the burger a quarter turn on the second side. Transfer the burgers to a wire rack, cover, and let rest.

4 Butter the inside of the buns and place them buttered-side down on a griddle or cast-iron skillet set over medium-high heat. Toast until golden, 2 to 3 minutes.

5 To build each burger, spread mustard over the bottom bun and top with onion and pickles. Top with the hamburger patty, then hot chili gravy, lettuce, and the top bun. Serve immediately.

POS-TRES

DESSERTS

CLASSIC CHURROS AND DULCE DE LECHE MILKSHAKE 204

HORCHATA RICE PUDDING WITH CHERRIES AND ALMONDS 209

PRALINES 207

TRES LECHES CAKE WITH TOASTED COCONUT 210

MEXICAN CHOCOLATE FLAN 213

SWEET PLANTAINS CON CAJETA 214

SOPAIPILLAS WITH LOCAL HONEY 217

PALETAS 218

AVOCADO, COCONUT, AND LIME | FRESAS CON CREMA | PINEAPPLE-TAJÍN

Growing up, THE ONLY THING I REMEMBER

eating for dessert after a Tex-Mex dinner was praline candy. Usually, by the time our family had finished a whole meal, we were way too full to even consider dessert, but a little praline was the perfect bite of sweetness to savor as we headed out to the car. If we ever actually ordered from the dessert menu, it was for special occasions. The options back then were pretty simple: flan (a Mexican version of crème caramel—see page 213) and sopaipillas (fried pastry dough doused in honey with a sprinkle of cinnamon—see page 217). It wasn't until later that desserts like *tres leches* and different ice creams began to find their way onto menus. The recipes in this chapter include both the old standbys and the newer sweets that are worth saving room for.

DULCE
DE LECHE
MILKSHAKE
PAGE 204

AND

CLASSIC CHURROS

CLASSIC CHUR

 SERVES 4

FOR THE ICE CREAM

1½ cups whole milk

1 cup heavy cream

2 teaspoons nonfat dry milk powder

1 vanilla bean, split lengthwise and seeds scraped out

8 large egg yolks

1 cup granulated sugar

¼ cup light corn syrup

½ teaspoon kosher salt

2 teaspoons vanilla extract

FOR THE DULCE DE LECHE

1 (14-ounce) can sweetened condensed milk

WHILE SOPAIPILLAS feel akin to the French beignet, the churro is very much reminiscent of the American doughnut—and it may just be the best of its kind. I love how the fluted grooves shelter extra clumps of cinnamon-sugar, thereby amplifying the crunchiness. While delicious on their own, they're best dipped in something. Melted chocolate is the standard sidekick, but here I've created a caramel-y blended ice cream that I think is like an amped-up Wendy's Frosty that's killer with the churros.

1 MAKE THE ICE CREAM In a medium saucepan set over medium-high heat, combine the milk, cream, milk powder, and vanilla bean seeds. Bring to a simmer. Remove the pan from the heat.

2 In a medium bowl, whisk together the egg yolks, granulated sugar, and corn syrup until the mixture is thick and pale yellow, 2 to 3 minutes. While whisking continuously, gradually add half the hot milk mixture, 1 tablespoon at a time, to the egg mixture to temper the eggs. Pour the egg mixture into the saucepan with the remaining milk mixture and set over medium-high heat. Cook, stirring continuously, until the mixture reaches 180°F on a candy thermometer, 3 to 4 minutes. Remove the pan from the heat and stir in the salt and vanilla extract. Pour the mixture through a fine-mesh strainer into a heat-safe container. Cover and refrigerate overnight or until the mixture has chilled to 40°F, 4 to 5 hours.

3 MAKE THE DULCE DE LECHE Peel the label off the can of condensed milk. Place the sealed can in a large saucepan and cover with water by 2 inches. Set the pan over high heat and bring the water just to a boil. Reduce the heat to the lowest setting possible and gently simmer for 3 hours. Be sure to add more water as needed to keep the can covered at all times.

ROS _and_ DULCE DE LECHE MILKSHAKE

FOR THE CHURROS

Vegetable oil, for frying

1 cup granulated sugar

2 teaspoons ground cinnamon

2 tablespoons shortening

2½ tablespoons packed light brown sugar

1 cup all-purpose flour

¼ teaspoon freshly grated nutmeg

½ teaspoon kosher salt

½ teaspoon vanilla extract

FOR THE MILKSHAKE

1 cup whole milk

4 Carefully remove the can from the water and let it cool to room temperature. Once cool, open the can and pour the condensed milk, which is now dulce de leche, into an airtight container and set aside at room temperature until ready to use.

5 When the ice cream base is chilled, transfer the mixture to an ice cream maker and process according to the manufacturer's directions. Transfer the ice cream to a freezer-safe container, cover, and freeze until ready to use.

6 **MAKE THE CHURROS** Fill a Dutch oven or other heavy pot with oil to a depth of 1 inch. Heat the oil over medium-high heat to 375°F. Line a wire rack with paper towels, place it on a baking sheet, and set it nearby.

7 Combine the granulated sugar and cinnamon in a large bowl. Set aside.

8 In a medium saucepan set over medium-high heat, combine the shortening, brown sugar, and 1 cup water. Bring to a boil, stirring occasionally. Remove the pan from the heat and add the flour, nutmeg, salt, and vanilla extract all at once. Beat with a wooden spoon to form a soft dough. Transfer the dough to a piping bag fitted with a star tip.

9 Carefully pipe a 6-inch piece of dough into the hot oil and cook, basting with the oil and turning, until golden brown on all sides, 3 to 4 minutes. Using a slotted spoon, transfer the churro to the prepared rack to drain for 1 minute. Toss in the cinnamon-sugar mixture and set aside. Repeat to fry the remaining batter.

10 **MAKE THE MILKSHAKE** Scoop 4 cups of the ice cream into a blender and add the milk and ½ cup of the dulce de leche. Blend until well combined and creamy, about 1 minute.

11 Divide the milkshake among four glasses and serve with the warm churros.

pralines

THERE REALLY ISN'T MUCH TO A GOOD PRALINE.
At a minimum it's simply brown sugar and pecans, though some recipes like to include things like evaporated milk, regular milk, and/or corn syrup. More important than the ingredients is the texture. A good Tex-Mex-style praline should be firm and a little brittle—not chewy like the pralines you find in the American South. There should be a snap when you bite into it, which should quickly be followed by the satisfaction of it melting in your mouth.

2 cups sugar

¾ cup whole milk

½ teaspoon baking soda

½ teaspoon vanilla extract

1 tablespoon unsalted butter

⅛ teaspoon kosher salt

2 cups pecan halves, toasted

Pinch of ground cinnamon

Pinch of Dutch-process cocoa powder

1   Line two baking sheets with parchment paper.

2   In a medium saucepan set over high heat, combine the sugar, milk, and baking soda. Bring to a boil, stirring occasionally. Cook the mixture until it reaches 235°F to 238°F on a candy thermometer, 4 to 6 minutes. Remove the pan from the heat. Let cool, without stirring, for 2 minutes.

3   Add the vanilla, butter, salt, and pecans and stir until the mixture begins to thicken and lighten in color, 3 to 4 minutes. Spoon heaping tablespoons of the mixture, ½ inch apart, onto the prepared baking sheets. Let the pralines cool completely.

4   The pralines will keep in an airtight container at room temperature for up to 1 week.

A BASKET OF
PRALINES

At most of the old-school Tex-Mex restaurants in days past, you never paid your bill at the table. Instead, you'd take your tab up to a cash register at the front of the restaurant, where someone—likely the owner or a general manager—would take your payment. It was a great moment in customer service, since that person would likely inquire how your meal was, and if you were a regular, you'd be engaged in a more personal conversation about how your family was doing. Invariably, there was a little basket of plastic-wrapped pralines for sale. They were more simply referred to as "candy," and for 50 cents a pop, they were an easy add-on to the bill. If you saw the smaller, more condensed ones in tight shrink-wrap, you knew they were probably commercially made. But if they were flat and loosely covered in colorful cling wrap, they were unquestionably made in-house. The latter were not to be missed: a perfect small bite of something sweet to complete the experience.

RICE PUDDING

WITH
CHERRIES AND ALMONDS

MAKES 4 ½-CUP PUDDINGS

I'VE ALWAYS LOVED THE TEXTURE OF RICE PUDDING. To me, it sort of takes the average custard experience to another level. This recipe takes my love for the humble dessert in a different direction using the flavors of horchata. The comforting vanilla and warm cinnamon are a perfect combination. This dish is balanced by the tart and sweet character of cherries and buttery toasted almonds.

FOR THE PUDDING

2 ¼ cups whole milk

½ cup short-grain white rice

½ cup sugar

1 cinnamon stick

½ teaspoon vanilla bean paste

⅛ teaspoon kosher salt

2 tablespoons sweetened condensed milk

Pinch of ground cinnamon

FOR THE CHERRY COMPOTE

¼ cup sugar

1½ teaspoons cornstarch

Pinch of kosher salt

3 tablespoons fresh orange juice

4 ounces fresh pitted cherries (defrosted frozen cherries are fine)

¼ teaspoon vanilla extract

¼ teaspoon cherry extract (optional)

FOR THE ALMONDS

¼ cup coarsely chopped almonds

4 tablespoons (½ stick) unsalted butter

Pinch of kosher salt

1 MAKE THE PUDDING In a medium saucepan set over medium heat, combine the milk, rice, ¼ cup of the sugar, the cinnamon stick, vanilla paste, and salt. Bring to a simmer. Reduce the heat to low, cover, and simmer until the rice is tender, 30 to 35 minutes.

2 Remove the pan from the heat and discard the cinnamon stick. Stir in the remaining ¼ cup sugar, the condensed milk, and the ground cinnamon. Transfer the mixture to a container and cover with a plastic wrap pressed directly against the surface of the pudding to prevent a film from forming. Refrigerate until chilled completely, about 3 hours.

3 MAKE THE COMPOTE In a small saucepan set over medium heat, whisk together the sugar, cornstarch, salt, orange juice, and 1 tablespoon water. Cook, stirring occasionally, until the sauce is thick and bubbling, 3 to 5 minutes. Stir in the cherries, vanilla extract, and cherry extract (if using) and cook, stirring occasionally, until the cherries are softened and warmed through, 2 to 3 minutes. Remove the pan from the heat and cover to keep warm.

4 MAKE THE ALMONDS In a medium nonstick skillet set over medium-high heat, combine the almonds and butter. Cook, stirring frequently, until the butter browns and the almonds are golden, 5 to 6 minutes. Drain the almonds in a strainer set over a bowl, reserving the browned butter, and transfer them to a paper-towel-lined plate. Sprinkle the almonds with the salt.

5 Divide the chilled pudding among four bowls. Top each with some of the warm compote, almonds, and a drizzle of the browned butter. Serve immediately.

TRES LECHES CAKE *with* TOASTED COCONUT

SERVES 12 TO 20

Tres leches means "three milks," which in this cake refers to the three different kinds of milk used to soak the white cake. It's definitely a decadent dessert for one of those special occasions. The spongy cake becomes heavy and moist as it barely manages to hold all the rich, sweet milks. With a topping of airy whipped cream and toasted coconut, it's a pretty special treat.

Cooking spray

8 large eggs

1½ cups sugar

½ cup all-purpose flour

1½ teaspoons vanilla extract

1 (14-ounce) can sweetened condensed milk

1 (5-ounce) can evaporated milk

3 cups heavy cream

1 cup unsweetened coconut flakes

TIP The cake needs to be refrigerated overnight before enjoying.

1 Preheat the oven to 300°F. Spray a 9 x 13-inch baking pan with cooking spray.

2 In the bowl of a stand mixer fitted with the whisk attachment, combine the eggs and 1 cup of the sugar. Beat on low speed until just combined, a few seconds. Increase the speed to high and beat until the mixture has doubled in volume, about 5 minutes. Reduce the speed to low and gradually add the flour, a little at a time, until it has all been incorporated. Add 1 teaspoon of the vanilla and beat to combine. Transfer the batter to the prepared pan.

3 Bake until the top of the cake is golden around the edges and a wooden pick inserted into the center of the cake comes out clean, about 1 hour. Transfer the cake to a wire rack and let cool in the pan for 30 minutes.

4 Using a skewer or a fork, poke holes all over the top of the cake all the way through to the bottom. Let cool completely.

5 In a large bowl, whisk together the condensed milk, evaporated milk, and 1 cup of the cream until well combined. Pour one-third of this mixture over the top of the cake and let the cake absorb the liquid, then repeat twice more, letting the cake absorb the liquid after each addition. Cover with plastic wrap and refrigerate overnight.

6 In the bowl of a stand mixer fitted with the whisk attachment, combine the remaining ½ cup sugar, 2 cups cream, and ½ teaspoon vanilla. Beat on medium-high speed until stiff peaks form. Spread the whipped cream evenly over the top of the cake. (If not serving immediately, cover the cake and store in the refrigerator for 1 to 2 days.)

7 When ready to serve, preheat the oven to 375°F.

8 Spread the coconut over a rimmed baking sheet. Toast in the oven, stirring every 2 to 3 minutes, until golden brown, 5 to 7 minutes. Transfer to a plate and let cool completely.

9 Slice and serve the cake immediately, sprinkling each slice with toasted coconut.

MEXICAN CHOCOLATE
Flan

½ cup sugar

3 large eggs

½ (14-ounce) can sweetened condensed milk

1 cup evaporated milk

½ teaspoon ground cinnamon

⅛ teaspoon ground allspice

¼ teaspoon kosher salt

1¾ ounces dark chocolate (55% to 64% cacao)

¼ teaspoon vanilla extract

Though flan is traditionally made with a vanilla custard, I love to switch things up and use Mexican chocolate, which has a mild cinnamon character. Flan is best when the caramel has had a chance to really develop on the bottom of the baking dish before it's inverted and served, so make sure to let it chill for a good long time (overnight really is best).

1 Place a rack in the center of the oven and preheat the oven to 300°F. Pour 1 inch of water into a large roasting pan and put it in the oven.

2 Place the sugar in a small saucepan set over medium-high heat. Cook, stirring continuously, until the sugar melts and becomes light amber in color, 6 to 8 minutes. Carefully divide the caramel among six 4-ounce ramekins, covering the bottom of each dish.

3 In a medium bowl, whisk the eggs and set aside.

4 In a medium saucepan set over medium-high heat, combine the condensed milk, evaporated milk, cinnamon, allspice, and salt. Bring just to a simmer, then remove the pan from the heat and stir in the chocolate until it has melted and the mixture is smooth.

5 While whisking continuously, slowly drizzle the hot milk mixture into the egg mixture. Add the vanilla and whisk to combine. Pour the custard through a fine-mesh strainer. Evenly divide the custard among the ramekins.

6 Carefully set the ramekins in the roasting pan of water in the oven. Bake until the custard is set around the edges but still jiggles slightly in the center, 35 to 40 minutes. Remove the ramekins from the roasting pan and let cool slightly. Cover and refrigerate overnight or until completely cold.

7 When ready to serve, run a knife around the edges of each ramekin to loosen the flan. Invert each ramekin onto an individual plate, getting as much of the caramel to drizzle out as you can.

8 Serve immediately.

Sweet Plantains CON CAJETA

SERVES 4

ON OCCASION I've seen a dessert of fried bananas at Tex-Mex restaurants. They're usually served dusted with cinnamon-sugar and sometimes come with a side of ice cream. It's a spin on the more traditional Mexican dessert of fried plantains served with a drizzle of Mexican crema. Personally, I think the starchy character of the plaintain is best paired with the caramel creaminess of the *cajeta*. Typically cajeta is made with goat's milk. This recipe uses sweetened condensed milk, but the thick, rich flavor of this version reminds me more of this favored Mexican caramel than the standard cow's milk dulce de leche, which is generally a little runnier in consistency.

1 (14-ounce) can sweetened condensed milk

Vegetable oil, for frying

4 very ripe plantains

1 Peel the label off the can of condensed milk. Place the sealed can in a large saucepan and cover with water by 2 inches. Set the pan over high heat and bring the water just to a boil. Reduce the heat to the lowest setting possible and gently simmer for 3 hours. Be sure to add more water as needed to keep the can covered at all times.

2 Carefully remove the can from the water and let it cool to room temperature. Once cool, open the can and pour the cooked condensed milk, which is now cajeta, into an airtight container and set aside at room temperature until ready to use.

3 Fill a Dutch oven or other heavy pot with oil to a depth of 2 inches. Heat the oil over medium-high heat to 365°F.

4 Peel the plantains and cut them on an angle into 4 even pieces each. Carefully add the plantains to the hot oil, 8 pieces at a time, and fry until the plantains are brown and crispy on the outside and very tender on the inside, 6 to 7 minutes. Using a slotted spoon, transfer them to a paper-towel-lined plate. Repeat to fry the remaining plaintains.

5 Place the warm plantains on a plate, drizzle with the cajeta, and serve immediately.

SOPAIPILLAS
with LOCAL HONEY

SERVES 8 TO 10

LIGHT AND AIRY, sopaipillas are probably second to pralines in terms of the most commonly served Tex-Mex desserts. (Flan would be a close third.) I used to think they were just flour tortillas fried until puffy clouds and drizzled with honey and cinnamon—maybe some of them actually were. Later I learned that they're made from a particular dough that's similar to beignet dough. They require less of a commitment for those wanting a little something sweet after a big meal than other, more involved treats. Plus, there's something so satisfying about popping them with a fork and watching the steam escape from the chewy dough.

MAKES 25 TO 30 (2-INCH) SOPAIPILLAS

2 tablespoons unsalted butter

1 cup sugar

2 teaspoons ground cinnamon

½ teaspoon ground mace or freshly grated nutmeg

4 cups bread flour, plus more for dusting

2 teaspoons baking powder

1½ teaspoons kosher salt

2 tablespoons cold lard (see page 24), or vegetable shortening

1½ cups warm water

Vegetable oil, for greasing and frying

Honey (preferably local), for drizzling

1 Cut the butter into ¼-inch pieces and freeze for 10 minutes.

2 In a large bowl, combine the sugar, cinnamon, and ¼ teaspoon of the mace. Set aside.

3 In a large bowl, combine the flour, baking powder, salt, and remaining ¼ teaspoon mace. Add the chilled butter and the lard and work them into the flour mixture with your fingers until the fat is the size of small peas. Add the warm water and mix with your hands until the dough pulls away from the sides of the bowl and forms a ball. Rub the inside of a clean large bowl with oil and transfer the dough to the bowl. Cover the dough with plastic wrap and set aside at room temperature to rest for 25 minutes.

4 Fill a Dutch oven or other heavy pot with oil to a depth of 1 inch. Heat the oil over high heat to 375°F. Line a wire rack with paper towels, place it on a baking sheet, and set it nearby.

5 Meanwhile, transfer the dough to a lightly floured surface and, using a rolling pin, roll it out to a ¼-inch thickness. Cut the dough into 2-inch squares.

6 Carefully place 3 or 4 pieces of dough at a time into the hot oil and cook, stirring gently, until golden brown, 4 to 5 minutes. Using a slotted spoon, transfer them to the prepared rack to drain for 2 to 3 minutes before tossing them in the sugar mixture. Repeat to fry the remaining dough.

7 Serve the sopaipillas warm with a drizzle of honey.

PALETAS

THESE ARE NOT ORDINARY ICE POPS.
A traditional Mexican sweet, fruit pops can be made with any seasonal fruit, and they're super refreshing and virtually guilt-free. At Superica, we took the idea of the *paleta* and made an orange push-pop dessert. We give them out to kids as a bonus treat, but I've seen plenty of parents treating themselves to one or two when they think no one is looking—I can't say I blame them. Here are three of my favorite varieties of frozen pops.

AVOCADO, COCONUT, AND LIME
Makes 8 ice pops

4 large avocados, pitted and peeled
1 (8 ½-ounce) can cream of coconut (I like Coco López)
Zest of 1 lime
½ cup fresh lime juice
Pinch of kosher salt

1 In a blender, combine the avocados, coconut cream, lime zest, lime juice, salt, and ½ cup water and purée until smooth, about 1 minute. Pour into ice pop molds and freeze until solid, at least 6 hours. The paletas will keep in the freezer for 3 to 4 weeks.

TIP Tajín is a Mexican seasoning primarily known for its chile and lime flavor. It can be found at specialty Latin markets and online.

FRESAS CON CREMA
Makes 8 ice pops

1 pound fresh strawberries, hulled
¼ cup sugar
1 tablespoon fresh lemon juice
¼ cup sweetened condensed milk

1 In a blender, combine the strawberries, sugar, and lemon juice and purée until smooth, about 1 minute. Transfer the mixture to a medium bowl, add the condensed milk, and stir briefly, just until the milk is swirled through the strawberry mixture—do not completely combine. Pour the mixture into ice pop molds and freeze until solid, at least 6 hours. The paletas will keep in the freezer for 3 to 4 weeks.

PINEAPPLE-TAJÍN
Makes 8 ice pops

¼ cup sugar
1½ pounds chopped fresh pineapple
2 teaspoons Tajín seasoning (see Tip)

1 In a small saucepan set over high heat, combine ¼ cup water and the sugar. Cook, stirring frequently, until the sugar has dissolved, 3 to 4 minutes. Remove the pan from the heat and let cool until the syrup is no longer steaming, 10 to 15 minutes.

2 In a blender, combine the cooled syrup and the pineapple and purée until almost smooth, leaving some small pieces of pineapple intact. Pour the purée into ice pop molds and evenly sprinkle with Tajín. Freeze until solid, at least 6 hours. The paletas will keep in the freezer for 3 to 4 weeks.

THE SWEET SOUND OF THE
PALETERO

Most people throughout the United States have some memory of the neighborhood ice cream man meandering the streets in a refrigerated truck, blaring a repetitive jingle from a hood-mounted megaphone. Though the music was a bit of an ear worm, in the summertime, it signified the sweet prospect of a frozen treat—assuming you could finagle a bit of spare change from your mom, the kitchen junk drawer, or the cushions of the couch.

Growing up in Texas, we had plenty of ice cream trucks that would circle our suburban streets, but I also get a pang of nostalgia when I hear the jingle-jangle of bells that dangle from the handlebars of a wheelbarrow-size pushcart that carries a cooler of Mexican ice cream and fruit ice pops, or *paletas*. The man pushing the cart is typically called a *paletero*, but to most kids, he's pretty much a superhero.

At the sound of his simple little bells, kids gather from all around to peer into his cooler of treats. Usually he has a few American selections, like sundae cones and push pops, but he also offers traditional Mexican *bolis* (freeze pops encased in a plastic tube like Otter Pops) and *paletas* in a variety of fresh-fruit flavors like mango, pineapple, and strawberry, as well as Mexican chocolate, coconut, and *arroz con leche* (rice and sweet milk).

You can still find *paleteros* in San Antonio, Houston, and towns throughout the Lower Rio Grande Valley. And while it's been ages since I've run into one, I guarantee I'd be the first in line if I heard the jingling nearby.

BEB-IDAS

DRINKS

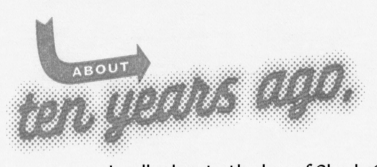

ABOUT *ten years ago,*

I walked up to the bar of Shady Grove restaurant in Austin to get a drink. The bartender smiled and greeted me, but instead of asking me if I wanted a cocktail, he asked, "Can I get you a margarita?" as if that was the standard order, which it likely was. And that was when it hit me that the margarita has become so standard, so fundamental in Tex-Mex culture, that it's about as obvious to the experience as chips and salsa. It's not unusual to find restaurants with an entire drink menu devoted just to margaritas, with various flavors, tequila selections, and presentations. But while the frosty tequila-and-lime beverage is delicious, Tex-Mex is not, in fact, a one-cocktail cuisine. Palomas, *micheladas*, various sangrias, and other cocktails have come to the fore in recent years, and for good reason—they're all tasty and hit different notes for different moods. If you ask me, the more, the merrier. In this chapter, I share recipes for a variety of beverages, as well as paying homage to the revered margarita.

SANGRIA
PAGE 241

CLASSIC MARG

SERVES 1

Kosher salt, for rim (optional)

Ice

3 ounces reposado tequila

2 ounces Cointreau

1½ ounces fresh lime juice

½ ounce Simple Syrup (recipe follows)

Fresh lime wheel, for garnish

THE KEY TO A GOOD MARGARITA is good tequila. In higher-quality tequilas, the sweet character of the agave shines through and you don't need to add as much sugar or simple syrup to the cocktail. Fresh lime juice is a must, as is a good-quality orange liqueur like Cointreau or Royal Combier. Served on the rocks with a salt-rimmed glass is the way to go, in my opinion.

1 If you like, dip the edge of a rocks glass in water and then in the salt to coat. Fill the glass with ice and set aside.

2 Fill a cocktail shaker with ice and add the tequila, Cointreau, lime juice, and simple syrup. Cover and shake well for 30 seconds. Strain into the prepared rocks glass. Garnish with the lime wheel and serve.

SIMPLE SYRUP

MAKES ABOUT 3/4 CUPS

½ cup sugar

½ cup water

In a small saucepan over medium-high heat, combine the sugar and water. Heat until the sugar has completely dissolved, 2 to 3 minutes. Remove from the heat and let cool. Store in the refrigerator in an airtight container for 3 to 4 weeks.

ARITA
on the ROCKS

SO LET'S SAY YOU LIKE YOUR MARGARITAS FROZEN, but you don't have the luxury of owning a commercial-grade frozen margarita machine.

Considering that not all home blenders are created equal, it's difficult to offer a foolproof recipe for the perfect frozen margarita. But there is a great alternative I like to make at home that gets all the margarita ingredients super cold and makes a nice frothy drink that's just as enjoyable as the real deal.

Simply throw the ingredients from the Classic Margarita on the Rocks into a blender along with ½ cup ice. Blend until the ice is broken down to a slushy consistency and the drink is frothy. Pour into a rocks glass filled with ice and serve immediately.

If you're entertaining, you can easily batch this recipe based on the number of people you're serving.

THE LEGEND OF THE
MARGARITA

The origin of the margarita has been a topic of dispute for decades. While the first written recipe for the cocktail was published in *Esquire* magazine in 1953, it's hard to pin down where the now ubiquitous tequila-and-lime beverage first appeared. One story claims that it's the namesake cocktail of a Dallas socialite, Margarita Dames, who used to hold extravagant parties at her lavish villa in Acapulco. Other tales attribute the cocktail's creation to the Rancho La Gloria restaurant just south of Tijuana, which was popular in the mid-1930s, and whose owner Danny Herrera made this drink for one of his regular customers who was partial to tequila.

And then many others believe the storied cocktail comes from the Agua Caliente hotel in Tijuana, which was frequented by many Hollywood stars in the early twentieth century. A beautiful young dancer by the name of Margarita Carmen Cansino was one of the hotel's main attractions, and an enamored bartender at the hotel created a cocktail in her name. Cansino would go on to great international fame under the stage name Rita Hayworth.

Considering a basic margarita is a simple three-ingredient cocktail, it's not hard to imagine that it was probably mixed up by a number of people before it ever became famous. In all likelihood, the margarita was probably created sometime during Prohibition, when many affluent Americans along the Southwest border states would head over to Mexico for guilt-free libations. However it was created, it's delicious and will always have a home on the Tex-Mex table.

THE "EL JEFE" MARGARITA

AUSTIN'S Cedar Door bar claims the honor of inventing the Mexican Martini, a twist on the standard margarita. It arrives in a frosty metal shaker and is accompanied by a chilled glass adorned with two fat green olives impaled on a toothpick. At Superica, we call it the El Jefe and serve it with a wheel of lime instead of the olive. Be warned: Mix up a second serving at your own risk—these babies will knock you on the floor. As with the margarita, keep everything chilled hours before you shake it all together, and that includes the martini glass.

Kosher salt, for rim (optional)

Ice

3 ounces reposado tequila

1½ ounces fresh lime juice

¾ ounce agave nectar

Fresh lime wheel, for garnish

1 If you like, dip the edge of a martini glass in water and then in salt to coat. Fill the glass with ice and set aside.

2 Fill a cocktail shaker with ice. Add the tequila, lime juice, and agave. Cover and shake well. Strain into the prepared martini glass. Garnish with the lime wheel and serve.

THE RUBY SWEET AND RIO STAR

In recent years, the Paloma has risen in popularity as an alternative to the classic margarita. But in Mexico, it has always been a favorite cocktail. I love the fresh grapefruit flavor of the Paloma, especially when made with a red grapefruit variety, which are a little sweeter than other grapefruit and have a beautiful fiery pink-and-orange color.

Of course, we owe a lot to the Spanish and French for introducing the grapefruit to the United States in the early 1800s. While the citrus first found a home in Florida, it later made its way to Texas, where it flourished in the sunny subtropical climate and fertile soils of the Rio Grande Valley. It was there in the 1920s that a rich, red mutation of the fruit was discovered, and farmers quickly cultivated it into two patented varieties: the Star Ruby and the Rio Red. Today, they're marketed as Ruby Sweet and Rio Star, and when they're in season in the winter and spring, they have the most fantastic juice.

Texas Star PALOMA

SERVES 1

I'M ALWAYS GAME for a good margarita or an ice-cold Mexican beer, but I'll let you in on a little secret: My favorite cocktail is the Paloma. I love the freshness of the grapefruit mixed with tequila, and at Superica, we add elderflower liqueur for a little floral character. The best is when the grapefruit juice is bright pink from a juicy, in-season Star Ruby or Rio Red grapefruit (see page 237); try to find one of those, if you can, though a regular grapefruit works well, too.

Ice

1½ ounces Gran Centenario Rosangel hibiscus tequila

½ ounce St-Germain elderflower liqueur

1 ounce fresh grapefruit juice

½ ounce fresh lime juice

½ ounce Simple Syrup (page 228)

Lime wedge, for garnish

Fill a cocktail shaker with ice. Add the tequila, St-Germain, grapefruit juice, lime juice, and simple syrup and shake well. Strain into an old-fashioned glass filled with ice. Garnish with the lime wedge and serve.

SERVES
8

Sangria

THOUGH SANGRIA is from Spain, it has had a long-standing presence in Mexican and Tex-Mex cuisines. A lot of restaurants serve it as a way to sell through cheaper selections of wine, the result of which for the customer is usually a severe headache the next day. If you ask me, sangria should be treated with respect. And when blended to showcase seasonal fruit, the drink can be fantastic. The best thing about sangria is that it's a perfect cocktail to batch for entertaining a lot of people. The longer it can steep and let the fruit and other ingredients commingle, the better it is in the glass, so it's also great to make ahead of time. Just be sure you make enough—it always goes fast.

1 orange, peeled, seeded, and chopped

1 apple, cored and chopped

4 ounces brandy

4 ounces triple sec

⅓ cup sugar

4 ounces fresh orange juice

1 bottle red wine

Ice

Lemon-lime soda (optional)

1   In a 2-quart pitcher, combine the orange, apple, brandy, and triple sec. Set aside.

2   In a small saucepan set over medium-high heat, combine the sugar and ½ cup water. Heat, stirring, just until the sugar dissolves, 2 to 3 minutes.

3   Add the sugar mixture, orange juice, and wine to the pitcher and stir to combine. Cover and refrigerate for 6 to 8 hours before serving to allow the flavors to meld.

4   Pour the sangria into eight ice-filled glasses and add a splash of lemon-lime soda to each, if desired. Serve immediately.

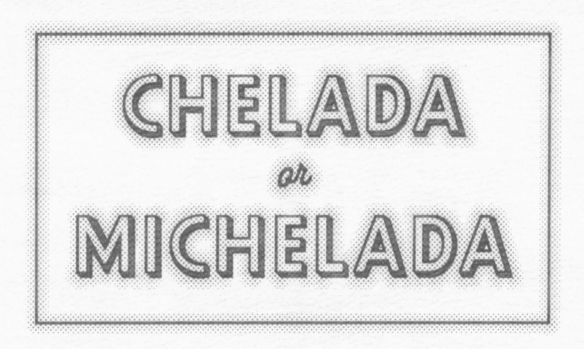

CHELADA or MICHELADA

I'VE BEEN ROUND AND ROUND on whether this refreshing beer cocktail is called a *chelada* or a *michelada*, and whether the two are the same drink or different ones. The term *chelada* means "a little cold one," while *mi–* makes the phrase possessive—"my little cold one." The drink starts with an ice-cold beer, which in my book is always a good beginning. From there, the only additions are a little salt and lime juice. While a lot of people believe it should include all the makings of a Bloody Mary, the truth is that only in some regions of Mexico do you find it ordered *con clamato*, or with tomato juice. In the States, I've typically seen the *chelada* listed on menus with just salt and lime, while *micheladas* tend to be listed with the other Bloody Mary ingredients, which is how we've included them here. It's really up to you to add what you want to add. Just make sure you've got a large cold glass to serve it in.

CHELADA
Serves 1

½ ounce fresh lime juice
Kosher salt
8 ounces Dos Equis Amber

1 Rub the rim of a frozen schooner glass with a small amount of the lime juice. Dip the rim into the salt to coat.

2 Pour the remaining lime juice into the glass, fill with ice, add the beer, and serve immediately.

MICHELADA
Serves 1

½ ounce fresh lime juice
½ ounce Bloody Maria Mix (page 244) or store-bought Bloody Mary mix
8 ounces Dos Equis Amber

1 Pour the lime juice and Bloody Maria Mix into a 12-ounce schooner glass and stir to combine.

2 Fill the glass with ice. Add the beer and serve immediately.

BLOODY
MARIA

SERVES 1

THOUGH I DO LOVE a Bloody Mary, I'm not much of a vodka fan, so I prefer to make them with good tequila for a variation called a Bloody Maria. But what makes a good Bloody Mary isn't the alcohol at all—it's the mix you use as the foundation. The ingredients need to be fresh and there needs to be a good amount of spice. For me the garnishes are what make this cocktail really fun. You can stay safe with your average celery stick and olives, but why not make it more interesting with pickled vegetables, spicy shrimp, or grilled chorizo? After one or two with garnishes like these, you don't need brunch. You've already had a whole meal.

Ice
4 ounces Bloody Maria Mix (recipe at right)
1½ ounces el Jimador tequila
Pickled jalapeño pepper slice, store-bought or homemade (page 62), for garnish
Lime wedge

Fill a collins glass with ice. Add the Bloody Maria Mix and tequila. Stir to combine. Garnish with the jalapeño and lime wedge. Serve immediately.

BLOODY MARIA MIX

MAKES ABOUT 5 CUPS

1 (28-ounce) can whole peeled tomatoes
¼ cup plus 3 tablespoons fresh lemon juice
1 tablespoon brine from a jar of pickled jalapeño peppers
1 teaspoon Worcestershire sauce
1 teaspoon hot sauce
1 tablespoon prepared horseradish
1 teaspoon chopped canned chipotle chile in adobo
¼ teaspoon celery salt
¼ teaspoon freshly ground black pepper

In a blender, combine the tomatoes, lemon juice, jalapeño brine, Worcestershire, hot sauce, horseradish, chipotle, celery salt, black pepper, and 1 cup plus 2 tablespoons water and purée until smooth.

If not using immediately, store in an airtight glass container in the refrigerator for up to 1 week.

Vampire WEEKEND

ONCE YOU'VE BEEN EXPOSED to the deliciousness of Horchata (page 54), you'll try to think of all sorts of ways to incorporate it into everything. For breakfast, it's a fantastic addition to coffee, and when you want to use it in an adult beverage, it pairs perfectly with rum. You can use a white rum for a lighter drink, but I like it with aged or spiced rum, as in this cocktail, for a little more depth.

Ice

1½ ounces Kraken spiced rum

4 ounces horchata, store-bought or homemade (page 54)

1 piece fresh pineapple, for garnish

Freshly grated nutmeg, for garnish

Fill a tall glass with ice. Add the rum and horchata and stir to combine. Garnish with the pineapple and nutmeg and serve immediately.

THE

HIGHWAYMAN

SERVES 1

While tequila has long had its day in the sun, more recent cocktail trends have unearthed the mysteries and nuances of mezcal. Often robust and smoky in flavor, mezcal offers a fantastic complexity to cocktails. And when subbed for whiskey in the classic Old-Fashioned, it makes for a more intriguing beverage that's just as boozy but with a little more depth.

Ice
2 ounces Sombra mezcal
½ ounce Agave Honey Syrup (recipe at right)
4 dashes of Bitter End Mexican Mole bitters
Strip of orange peel
3 coffee beans, for garnish

Pour the mezcal, syrup, and bitters into an old-fashioned glass and stir to combine. Add ice to fill the glass and stir to chill. Squeeze the orange peel over the glass to express the oil and drop it into the glass. Add the coffee beans and serve immediately.

AGAVE HONEY SYRUP

MAKES 2 CUPS

1 cup agave nectar
½ cup honey
½ cup boiling water
4 coffee beans

Place the agave, honey, boiling water, and coffee beans in a glass jar with a tight-fitting lid. Shake to combine, and refrigerate overnight before using. The syrup will keep in the refrigerator for 3 to 4 weeks.

ACKNOWLEDGMENTS

FORD WOULD LIKE TO THANK

It's surreal thinking about how this book ever came to be. I'm often bewildered at the way things have come together in my life, but when I stop to think about it, I realize just how fortunate I've been to be surrounded by gracious, helpful, and passionate people. Through this pretty amazing journey, I have found that putting others first, and serving them well, has opened so many doors for me and my team to all do what we love. For me, it doesn't get any better than that.

Digging deep into my earliest moments of eating Tex-Mex food, I see a laid-back, fun-loving boy sitting in a booth at Felix Mexican Restaurant in Houston with his mom and dad. I owe my love for this cuisine to them. Without their love and encouragement in my life, I wouldn't be who I am today. Thanks, Mom and Dad!

The depth of my gratitude is equally as profound for my wife and kids, who keep me grounded and have loved and encouraged me through the long hours and late nights of restaurant life. I love you.

In this restaurant life, I've found a number of chefs and friends—many of whom have become as close as family—to whom I owe much of my success. And my Tex-Mex compatriot, Kevin "Maximize" Maxey, is a true brother. Kevin, this book is as much yours as it is mine. Thanks for all the time matching your memories with mine and getting all of it onto the plate.

I owe a super-big thanks to Amanda Englander and the whole Clarkson Potter crew for making amazing books and believing that this one belonged in your stable. Your passion and creativity absolutely inspire me. To my agent, Lisa Ekus, thank you for making the connection to Potter. And to Katie Williams, thank you for strategizing to put the best possible team together.

Working on this book meant I needed two important things: someone to translate my recipes to come alive (and work) in a home kitchen, and someone who could conjure up the right words to express my devoted passion not only for delicious food but for a regional cuisine that's part of the soul of every Texan—and a growing number of people beyond the Lone Star State. To my partner and lover of all things spicy, Tamie Cook: You tested and tested and tested these recipes, and I'm grateful for your diligence. You rock! And a huge thanks to my cowriter and fellow Texan, Jessica Dupuy, whose expertise on Texas history and culture along with her own personal memories combined in a way to truly express my voice and convey my heart for Tex-Mex cuisine; through this book, we're truly family.

To my boy Johnny Autry, Charlotte, and crew, your photographic vision totally brought me back to a time when old plastic-covered tables, fiberglass tortilla warmers, and oversize oval plates of smoking-hot cheese enchiladas, beans, and rice were all a Texas boy truly needed to be happy. Thank you for that. I loved every minute of it.

On a sentimental note, I wish I could tell the late Jim Goode in person, "Jim, thanks for being the best cook I know and inspiring me by your love for everything Texas." He left an indelible mark in Houston's restaurant story, and Texas cuisine altogether. May we one day toast with cold beers over the eternal combo plate in the sky.

And finally, a word of thanks to David Crowder, for reminding me that Tex-Mex isn't meant to be anything overly technical or special. For those who grew up on it, "It's just food!"

A heartfelt thanks to Ford Fry for his unshakable commitment to all things delicious — particularly with regards to Tex-Mex. Thank you for giving me a chance to tell your story. Thanks to my mom for letting me sit on the counter next to her as a baby while she baked; to my dad for mastering the grill with all manner of meats; to my native-Texan extended family for making Tex-Mex an integral part of our daily lives; and to Marilu for loving on my kids and giving me the real scoop on authentic Mexican fare. Thanks to Amanda Englander and Clarkson Potter for wanting to make this book a reality; David Hale Smith for guiding me along the path; Stacy Hollister for your keen eye; and Katie Williams for keeping Ford and me on task! And finally, a special thanks to Robb Walsh, Melissa Guerra, Gustavo Arellano, Lisa Fain, Patricia Sharpe, and Courtney Bond for paving the way in documenting the stories of Tex-Mex and giving me a deep and profound love for Texas, its history, and the food that defines its identity. Most important, to Myers, Gus, and Ashlyn: I love you.

Index

A NATIVE TEXAN, FORD FRY'S culinary style developed over many years of cooking across the country: from eating out with his family as a child in Texas to studying at the New England Culinary Institute in Vermont to working as a chef in Florida, Colorado, California, Texas, and Georgia. In 2007, Ford opened his first restaurant in Atlanta: JCT. Kitchen, a seasonally inspired neighborhood restaurant focused on new Southern cooking. He later spread his commitment to local ingredients and friendly service to other chef-driven restaurants in Atlanta and in his native Houston. But in 2014, Fry honed in on the one cuisine that connected him most to his Texas roots: Tex-Mex. He opened The El Felix, a casual neighborhood Tex-Mex joint, in Atlanta, and it set him on a renewed mission in life: to bring true Tex-Mex beyond the borders of Texas. In 2015, he dug even deeper with the opening of Superica, an Austin-inspired Tex-Mex joint with two locations in Atlanta. He has since expanded Superica to Charlotte, and all the way back home to Houston, which, for Fry, is where it all began. He lives in Atlanta with his wife and children.

JESSICA DUPUY is a cookbook author and magazine writer—and also a native Texan. She has collaborated on many cookbooks, including James Beard Award-winning chef Tyson Cole's *Uchi: The Cookbook; The Salt Lick Cookbook: A Story of Land, Family and Love; Jack Allen's Kitchen Cookbook;* and *Southern Living* magazine's *The United Tastes of Texas* and *The United Tastes of the South.* She is a regular contributor to *Texas Monthly* magazine, *Imbibe* magazine, SevenFifty Daily, and numerous other regional publications. She is a member of Les Dames D'Escoffier and lives in Austin with her family.